Sight and Insight
—— Life in Lijiang, Baidi, and Yongning
Ulli Steltzer

我眼中和心中的形象
——生活在丽江、白地、永宁的人们

乌利·斯特尔兹 著　　菱蔓 安利 译

云南美术出版社

序

杨福泉

在中国云南、四川和西藏三省区毗邻的金沙江、澜沧江流域，在海拔5596米的玉龙大雪山下，有一个"纳西古王国"，这个古国的主体居民是纳西族，以及彝、藏、普米族等民族。纳西人分布在云南省丽江、宁蒗、永胜、中甸、德钦、鹤庆、剑川、兰坪、贡山，四川省的盐源、盐边、木里、巴塘以及西藏自治区的察隅、芒康等县，居住区大约在东经98.5～102度、北纬26.5～30度之间。纳西人所居住的区域平均海拔为2700米，境内多大山深谷，如玉龙雪山、哈巴雪山、白马雪山、贡嘎岭、虎跳峡等是闻名遐迩的名山大峡，是充满神秘气息的旅游探险之地。

绝大多数纳西人自称"纳西"(naxi)，有一部分自称"纳恒"(nahi)、"纳罕"(nahai)。"纳"(na)，在汉古文献中则称为"麽些"(读 mo-so)、"摩沙"、"摩梭"等。1954年，经中华人民共和国国务院批准，统一称为纳西族①。据1990年中国第四次人口普查，纳西族总人口为278009人，其中以滇西北的丽江县为最大的集聚区，当地的纳西族有184894人，占纳西族总人口的66%。

纳西语属于汉藏语系藏缅语族彝语支（近来有的语言学家又认为纳西族语言处于羌语支与彝语支分界点上，与这两种语言都密切相关），划分为以丽江坝区为代表的西部方言和宁蒗县永宁为代表的东部方言。

纳西族有本族宗教祭司——"东巴"用来书写经书的两种古老文字，一种是图画象形文字，纳西语称之为"斯究鲁究"(serjelvje)，意思是"木石上的痕记"（又译为"木石之标记"或"木石之记录"）。从文字形态看，东巴象形文是一种正从图画字向象形字过渡的文字，由于至今还有祭司东巴能识读和运用这种文字，因此国际上一些学者称为"世界上惟一保留完整的活着的象形文字"。另一种文字叫"哥巴"(ggeqbbaq)，它是一种表词文字(Phonetic script)，当文字记录语言时严格保持字和词相对应。一个字代表一个音节。

较多的学者认为纳西族渊源于远古时期居住在中国西北甘肃、青海的河（黄河）、湟（湟水）地带的古羌人(ancient Qiang People)，约从春秋战国(公元前770—221年)时起，陆续迁徙到现在所居住的区域。但随着纳西族分布地区各种考古实物的不断发现，一些学者提出了纳西族是南迁的古羌人与土著融合而形成的观点。

在古代，丽江纳西族曾有"梅"、"禾"、"束"、"尤"4个氏族，东部方言区的纳西族多数属纳西古氏族"梅"、"禾"两支后裔，西部方言区的纳西族多数属纳西古氏族"束"、"尤"两支后裔。在丽江、维西等地的纳西族中，家族之上的氏族组织早已消失。

纳西族中的家族组织很普遍，家族由几户至若干户共尊一个始祖的血缘亲属组成。在丽江、维西、中甸等实行一夫一妻制的纳西族地区，家族"崇窝"(co-o)依照父系血统而组成。结婚一般都要经过订亲、请新娘、举行婚礼的程序。同姓不同宗的人可以通婚，但同一"崇窝"之间禁止通婚。

泸沽湖地区纳人(naq)（即如今普遍所称的"摩梭"）的亲族组织保持着比较古老的特征，他们有母系家族组织"斯日"，后来母系家族逐渐分裂演变为母系家庭。到二十世纪50年代前，"斯日"内部各家之间的经济联系已经不多。纳人（摩梭）把母系氏族叫做"尔"，直至二十世纪60年代，永宁纳人的绝大多数家户还能说出自己分别属于"西"、"牙"、"胡"、"俄"4个古氏族。

泸沽湖地区的纳人（摩梭）中同时存在着母系家庭、母系父系并存家庭和父系家庭3种形式，但母系家庭是主要的家庭形式。母系家庭所有成员的世系皆从母，男女成员由一个或几个始祖母的后裔组成，母系血缘是维系家庭的基础，财产按母系继承，由母亲传给子女，舅传给甥和甥女。男子在家中的身份是舅祖、舅舅、兄弟、母亲的儿子或舅舅的外甥。每个母系家庭有一个家长，通常由年长或能干的妇女担任。舅掌礼仪、母掌财产是家庭权利和分工的形式。母系家庭的传统观念认为：女子是根种，缺了就断根。如果某个家庭一旦没有女继承人，便要过继养女或养子。

纳人（摩梭）与其母系家庭相应的婚姻形式是"阿夏"走访婚，"阿夏"在纳人语中意为"情侣"。"阿夏"婚的基本形式是男不娶女不嫁，相恋钟情者互相送信物定情。情侣双方都终身生活在母亲家里，男子在夜间到情侣家过偶居生活，次日黎明即返回自己的母亲家里。男女缔结"阿夏"关系要遵守传统习俗，只有不属于同一母系血缘的成年男女才能建立这种关系，"阿夏"所生的子女随母，血统也依母系计算。

纳西族有自己的本土宗教(indigenous Religion)，祭司的自称是"本补"(biubuq)或"本"(bu)——"本"有祭祀、诵经之意，民间称之为"东巴"，"东巴"意为"智者"、"老师"。因祭司被称为"东巴"，因此纳西本土宗教被称为东巴教。在纳西东部方言区，对本土宗教祭司称为"达巴"。达巴无象形文字经书，但口诵经很多。

东巴教源于纳西族古代巫教(Shamanism)，后来逐渐吸收了藏族的苯教(Bon)、藏传佛教等的一些内容，形成了一种独具特色的民族宗教。它有严密复杂的祭仪系统，庞大的鬼神体系，与各种仪式配套的象形文经书。泛灵信仰、自然崇拜、祖先崇拜、生命崇拜、重占卜、强调人与自然的和谐关系是东巴教的主要特征。东巴经中说，人类与大自然是兄弟俩，如果人与自然相互依存的和谐关系遭到破坏，就会引来灾难。因此，纳西族民间有很多保护自然生态的习惯法，以此规范制约着人们对待自然界的行为。东巴教的主要仪式"祭署"的主旨即是阐释人与自然之间相依互存的关系。祭司东巴熟谙纳西民情风俗、能歌舞、善书画，他们用自制的竹笔所写下的图画象形文古籍，中国学术界称之为"东巴经"，在西方国家一般称为Naxi Manuscripts（纳西手写本）。其内容包括宗教、历史、民俗、文学艺术、医学、天文、历法、地理、动植物、生产知识等，留存至今者多达1400种、20000多卷，分别收藏于丽江、昆明、南京、北京、台湾和美、德、英、法、意大利等国的博物馆和图书馆中。东巴经堪称纳西族古代百科全书。

纳西人还信仰汉传佛教、藏传佛教和道教。公元14～15世纪，纳西族木氏土司（Headman Family Mu）在云南、四川纳西族和藏族地区大力弘扬藏传佛教噶玛噶举教派（白教），建了很多寺庙，如著名的"滇西十三大寺"。如今在丽江还有属于该教派的指云、玉峰、文峰、普济、福国5大寺庙。在16世纪的明万历年间，木氏土司还主持刻印了著名的藏文《大藏经》，史称丽江版《甘珠尔》，这是在藏区正式第一次雕版的《大藏经》。永宁的纳人（摩梭）普遍信仰藏传佛教的格鲁巴教派（黄教），在公元1556年建立了著名的黄教扎美戈寺。道教传入纳西族地区后，产生了道教组织洞经会和皇经会，后来不少洞经会和皇经会逐渐演变为民间群众性的音乐娱乐组织，很多普通民众也成为洞经和皇经乐会的成员。演奏洞经音乐成为纳西族民间一种普遍的文娱活动。

纳西族对诸种宗教文化兼收并蓄的开放精神不仅促进了社会和经济的发展，也促成了艺术的繁荣。一些体现多元文化融合的艺术杰作由此产生，如著名的丽江白沙壁画即是明代丽江纳西族社会大开放的产物。白沙壁画最为突出的特点是表现在题材上的多种宗教和同种宗教中的各种教派内容相互融合并存，以及多民族的绘画技法揉为一体的现象。该壁画把汉传佛教、藏传佛教、道教的神佛绘于同一幅画中，突出地反映了纳西族在历史上善于吸纳多元的异民族文化，不偏执于一种宗教文化的特点。

著名的"丽江古乐"也是多元文化相融汇的艺术结晶。"丽江古乐"由"白沙细乐"和丽江洞经音乐、皇经音乐组成（"白沙细乐"今已濒于消亡，皇经音乐今已失传）自二十世纪40年代以来，很多音乐史家对"白沙细乐"这套组曲进行了研究，认为它是我国屈指可数的几部大型古典管弦乐之一，除历史悠久之外，其珍贵之处还在于它是丝竹合奏，分章节（尚存八首歌、舞、乐结合而成的套曲），其旋律与"和声"的独特是中国所仅见的，被誉为"活的音乐化石"。"丽江洞经音乐"是区别于中国各地道教音乐体系的艺术珍品。其所以珍贵，是因该乐还保留了一部分在中原早已失传的辞、曲音乐，如唐代的《浪淘沙》《紫微八卦舞（曲）》，元代的"北曲"等。近几年，丽江古乐越来越受到国内外旅游者和专家学者的欢迎，多次到北京、昆明等地演出；1995年和1997年，丽江大研古乐队应邀在英国、香港演出；1998年，该乐队应挪威国王之邀赴挪威演出。此后，又分别赴意大利、英国、德国、美国、瑞士等国演出。

性别是纳西族家庭劳动分工的基础，纳西男子主要从事劳动强度较大的犁田、挖田、耙地、播种、砍木料、劈石头、狩猎、砍柴、到高山放牛、制作农具以及皮革和铜器等传统工艺品、赶马运输、外出经商等；女子从事栽秧、砍柴、拉松毛、薅锄、收割、放羊、放猪、舂米磨面、做传统食品、到集市上出售生产品等。在城区，开铺子和摆摊做生意的多是妇女。纳西族妇女以勇敢、吃苦耐劳、不怕死而著称。从纳西族的传统来看，妇女的社会地位是比较高的，纳西族民间最大的节日"祭天"是祭纳西族女始祖的父母亲和舅舅（相传他们都是天神）。古代重女性，重母性的文化特征也反映在纳西语中，如纳西语中以"女"为大，以"男"为小，以"母"为大，以"子"为小。如祖房、大房称为"女房"、"母房"，小房称为"男房"、"子房"，一切大的东西多以"女"、"母"为词头。在一些固定词组中，女性在前，男性在后，如夫妻称为"尼奴阿改汝"（ninvegaissee），妻"尼奴"（ninv）在前，夫"阿改汝"（egaissee）在后。纳西族十分崇拜女神，相传东巴教神圣的占卜书是从盘祖萨美女神那里求来的，永宁纳人（摩梭）每年都有祭拜女神的节日。从古至今，纳西族妇女能调解部落、村寨、家族、邻里之间的纷争和矛盾。纳西族妇女的服饰——羊皮披肩背面缀有七块五彩丝线绣成的圆盘，象征日月星辰，其中寓有她们披星戴月地辛勤劳作的含义。二十世纪40年代留居丽江8年的俄裔作家顾彼德（Goullart.P.）在他所写的《被遗忘的王国》（Forgotten Kingdom）中这样写纳西妇女："她们是家庭的智囊，是家庭繁荣昌盛的依赖。与一个纳西女子结婚就相当于有了人生的保险，使人可以闲适舒服地度过余生。"（"They were the brains of the family and the only foundation of prosperity in the household. To marry a Nakhi woman was to acquire a life insurance, and the ability to be idle for the rest of one's days."）

纳西男人豪放爽朗而沉毅笃厚，过去是以强悍善战、勇猛无畏而著称的武士，后来有很多男子迷上文学艺术，喜欢养花，汉文书法、绘画、演奏音乐等。很多纳西人的庭院像个小花园，堂屋里多挂书法绘画作品，很多偏僻的山村里也不乏饱学之士。过去丽江每个乡村、城中的每条街道都有民众自发组织的古乐队，在繁忙的劳作之余吹拉弹唱，自得其乐。现在丽江城乡各地仍有十多个纳西古乐队，业余参加古乐队自娱的纳西人有教师、职员、大学生、工人、农民、商贩、屠夫等。由于纳西族有如此丰富的传统文化和很多温文儒雅的读书人，纳西族被很多人誉为"文化的民族"。此外，不少纳西男子是出色的工匠，他们生产的铜器和皮革制品远近有名。

公元1723年（清朝雍正元年），清朝政府在中国西南少数民族地区实行"改土归流"，实施"以夏变夷"的政策，封建政府向丽江纳西族社会全面灌输"三纲五常"的观念，强制性地改革纳西族的风俗，强化包办婚姻，纳西妇女被"三从四德"的封建礼教所羁绊。在丽江，各种带有极浓的封建色彩的重男轻女习俗不断形成，妇女受到重重压迫。

由于外来封建礼教文化、政治体制与纳西本土文化之间的激烈冲突等多种原因，在二十世纪50年代以前，无以计数的纳西情侣少则一对，多则数对乃至十对地为爱情、为反抗封建包办婚姻而殉情。他（她）们雍容盛装，在可以见到玉龙雪山的草深林密、风景优美之处，唱一曲悲风泣雨的殉情长歌"游悲"，含笑赴死。这种历史性的爱情大悲剧使丽江蒙上了"世界殉情之都"的凄婉哀伤之名，并酝酿出一个爱情乌托邦灵界(spiritual paradise)——"玉龙第三国"，相传它就在那座被纳西人视为神山，至今尚未被人类征服的玉龙大雪山上。他们相信那里是"白鹿当耕牛，红虎当坐骑，獐子当家狗，野鸡当晨鸡；青草当床铺，白云做被盖；晨雾为纱帐，日月做明灯，爱情无羁绊，青春永不逝；没有苦和痛，没有愁和泪"的大自然乐园。我从多年的调查中得知，在过去所有殉情悲剧发生的地区，女性殉情者都远远多于男性。女子比男子更倾向于殉情，殉情的决心也比男子更为坚定，这是因为孔孟封建礼教对妇女的压迫比男性深重的原因，同时，也与纳西族妇女"勇敢而不畏死"的传统精神有关。

中国历史文化名城——丽江大研古城地处极远的滇西边地，过去是纳西古王国的首府，著名的滇藏贸易"茶马古道"的要塞，城中的绝大多数居民是纳西人。该城典型地反映了纳西人博采众长而形成的高超的建筑艺术，是中国建筑史上的一个奇观。古城座落在玉龙雪山下海拔2400米的高原台地上，始建于宋末元初（一说古城已形成于唐代，即当时的"三赕城"），总面积3.8平方公里。四方街是古城中心，4条干道呈经络状向四周延伸。道路随水溪的曲直而修建，房屋就地势的高低而组合。"城依水存，水随城在"是古城的一大特色。位于城北的黑龙潭为古城主要水源，潭水由北向南蜿蜒而下，至双石桥处被分为东、中、西3条支流，各支流再分为无数溪流，穿街过巷，入墙绕户，形成主街傍河、小巷临水，跨水筑楼，家家流水，户户垂杨的景象。四方街西侧的西河上设有活动闸门，居民利用西河与东河的高差冲洗街面。众多大小水流之上，造型各异的古老石桥、木桥多达350多座，使大研古城的桥梁密度居中国之冠。古城的街巷全部用红色角砾岩石（此种石头因雨后呈现色彩斑斓的5种颜色，民间称为五花石）铺成，有晴不扬尘，雨不积水的优点。丽江古城是一个活生生的城，而不是那种历史博物馆式的死城。它在中国是惟一一个居民以少数民族占大多数的历史文化名城，数万普通的纳西人每天休养生息其中，满目可见淳厚的民风民俗。1997年，经联合国世界文化遗产评委会评审通过，丽江大研古城列入"世界文化遗产名录"。

随着时代的发展，在现代化和城市文化的浪潮冲击下，纳西人的故土和文化也在发生变迁，本土传统文化在衰落，他们需要得到外界更多朋友的理解、帮助和支持，使"云之南"这个美丽古老的雪国能可持续地发展和繁荣。我的加拿大朋友，摄影家乌利博士不顾年迈体衰，多次深入到丽江、永宁纳西人地区，用她独到的慧眼和艺术表现力拍摄了许多朴素、真实而动人的纳西人形象，我愿五洲四海的朋友们能从乌利的摄影作品中领略到当代纳西民众平和、宁静而纯朴的音容笑貌，在您有余暇之时，到这个美丽的"古代王国"来欣赏太古白雪、高山、大江和纳西人千百年的悲欢故事，来和纳西人交朋友。

（作者系云南省社会科学院副院长、研究员、博士）
2001年12月31日

---

① 丽江等地的纳西与永宁等地的纳人是同源异流的一个民族，国务院在1954年将该族族名统一定为"纳西族"。目前，宁蒗彝族自治县在自治条例中把摩梭（纳人）列为一个待识别的民族。本序言按目前国家统一的民族识别结论和对内对外宣传的惯例，将丽江等地的纳西人和永宁等地的纳人（摩梭）统一在纳西族中来论述。

Introduction
by Yang Fuquan

The ancient "Naxi Kingdom" is situated at the intersection of Yunnan, Sichuan, and Tibet, and area with an average elevation of 2700 meters, richly endowed with high snow-capped mountains, big rivers, and deep gorges. Most of its residents are of the Naxi nationality.

Old Chinese literature refers to the people of this kngdom as "Mo-so," "Mo-sha," or "Mo-suo." Today, however, most of their descendants call themselves "Naxi" (pinyin romanisation), though some call themselves "Naxi," "Nahai," or "Na." According to the 1990 national census, the Naxi nationality has a population of 278, 009, with 66% living in Lijiang County, the largest single region inhabited by the Naxi. The Naxi language, which belongs to the Sino-Tibetan language family, is divided into the western dialect, represented by the Naxi in the Lijiang Ba area, and the eastern dialect, represented by the Na (Mosuo) in the Yongning area, in Ninglang County.

Dayan town, the historic center of today's Lijiang city, is often referred to as the "Old Town." It was the capital of the ancient Naxi kingdom, a fortress on the Yunan-Tibet "Old Tea Trade Route." The town, which covers an area of 3.8 square kilometers at the foot of the Jade Dragon Snow Mountain, was built around the end of the 12th century, between the late Song and early Yuan Dynasties, Reviewed and approved by the United Nations World Cultural Heritage Committee in 1997, Lijiang Dayan is now listed as a "world cultural heritage site."

Lijiang is the only city in China where the majority population is an ethnic minority. Living here are tens of thousands of Naxi, whose habits and customs can be seen everywhere. The Black Dragon Pond, in the north, is the main water source. The water flows from north to south, divided into three tributaries, each tributary further divided into numerous streams moving through the town. Crossing the water are over 350 old stone bridges of various sizes and styles. The West river has a floodgate. The residents use the water level difference between the West and the East river to wash the streets, which are paved with large "five-blossom stones."

Traditionally, Naxi women are considered as brave, hardworking, undaunted by difficulties, and fearless of death. in the Naxi tradition, women have been given a higher social status than men. The greatest festival for the Naxi is the worship of heaven, which really means to worship the parents and brothers of a female ancestor. This old culture of looking up to women is also reflected in the language. For example, "big" is referred to as female or motherly, and "small" as male or of the son. In an ancestral house, big rooms are called female rooms and small rooms are called male rooms. In Naxi set phrases, the female element precedes the male element: a husband and wife is called "ninvegaissee" with "ninv," wife, preceeding "egaissee," husband.

In the past as well as the present, Naxi women may resolve any conflict and disagreement between tribes, villages, families and neighbors. The outfit of Naxi women -a shawl made from sheepskin and decorated with seven disks embroidered with five color silk symbolizing the sun, the moon and the stars- suggests that they work from morning till night. A Russian writer, Peter Goulart, who lived in Lijiang for eight years in the 1940's, wrote in his "Forgotten Kingdom" of the Naxi women:They were the brains of the family and the only foundation for prosperity in the household. To marry a Nakhi woman was to acquire life insurance, and the ability to be idle for the rest of one's days.

Naxi men are traditionally considered unconstrained and candid, steady and resolute, sincere and magnanimous. In the past, they were fearless warriors, full of valour and vigour. Later on, many became fascinated by literature, the art of growing flowers, Chinese calligraphy, drawing, painting and playing music. In old times, every village and every street in Lijiang communities had its own self-organized band whose members entertained themselves and others after a day's work by playing Naxi classical music. There are still over ten bands of this kind in Lijinag and surrounding villages. The band members include teachers, office workers, university students, farmers, business vendors, and even butchers.

Among the Naxi, the extended family is predonminant, consisting of several blood-related households that worship a common ancestor. In Lijiang, the family form of "co-o" is based on the father's blood lineage. "co-o" is an old Naxi word, "co" meaning "people" and "o" "bones," which roughly translates to "root-bone" and refers to several branches of descendants of a common ancestor. Naxi people regard the father's side of the family as "bones" and the mother's side of the family as "flesh."

In the Yongning and Lugu Lake areas, among the Na (Mosuo), there are three family types: patriarchal, matriarchal, and shared, with the matriarchal being the most popular. In that kind of family, all members are from the mother's side. Male or female, they are all descendants of one or several female ancestors. The blood relationship from the mother's side is the foundation of the family. Property is passed down from the mother's side: from the mother to her children, and from mother's brother to his sister's children.

A man's position in the family may be that of uncle, mother's brother, mother's cousin, son, or nephew. Every matriarchal family has a family head, an elderly or capable woman. The uncle takes charge of rituals; the mother takes care of finances. This is the normal form of distribution of rights and resposibilities in such families.

In a traditional matriarchal family, a young couple will not get married. Once in love, the man as well as the woman will continue to live in their own mothers' houses for life. The man will go to his lover's home for the night and return to his mother's home at dawn. This kind of relationship, often called a "walking marriage," is governed by old customs: only adult men and women from different blood families can be "lovers." Their children will live with the mother as part of their mother's blood family.

The Naxi nationality has its own indigenous religion. Their Shamans are referred to as "Dongba," which means "wise man" and "teacher." In Yongning, in the eastern dialect area, the Dongba is called "Ddaba." The Dongba religion originated from ancient Shamanism. It absorbed elements from the Tibetan Bon religion and Tibetan Buddhism to become a unique Naxi religion. It has a complex system of worshipping, a large assembly of gods and devils, and pictographic scriptures to go with each ceremony. The Dongba religion believes in harmonious relationships between humankind and nature, in pantheism and polytheism. It worships ancestry and life, and it emphasizes divination. Dongba scriptures say that man and nature are brothers. If their harmonious interdependence is damaged, disaster will follow. As a result, many Naxi customs are environmentally friendly.

Dongba shamans had a good knowledge of the Naxi people and their folk customs. They were accomplished at singing and dancing, painting and calligraphy. Their writing covers topics such as religion, history, folk customs, medicine, astronomy, the calendar, animals and plants, and production-related knowledge. Today more than 20,000 volumes of their pictographic writings may be found in libraries and museums around the world.

The Naxi have adopted an open attitude toward various religions and cultures. This has not only promoted social and economic development, but also the flourishing of the arts. The Baisha Murals, which were created in the Ming Dynasty, reflect this multi-culturalism. They depict the gods of Han Buddhism, Tibetan Buddhism, and Taoism coexisting in harmony. Another example of multi-cultural integration is the "Lijiang Classical Music," composed of "Baishaxiyue," Lijiang Dongjing Music, and Huangjing Music.

In 1723, the first year in the reign of Emperor Yongzheng in the Quing Dynasty, the government started a policy in southwest minority regions to "remold the region into the Chinese mainstream." The Naxi were forced to change their customs and ways of life to allow for arranged marriages, which led in time to the serious oppression of women. As a result of severe conflicts within Naxi culture, countless Naxi lovers-sometimes a single couple, sometimes as many as ten or more-would commit lovers' suicide, to protest arranged marriages. They would put on their best clothes, go to a beautiful place deep in the forest where they could see the Jade Dragon Snow Mountain, sing a last love song, and end their lives. This historic tragedy gave Lijiang the sad name of the "world capital for lovers' suicide".

It is believed that on that Jade Dragon Snow Mountain, there is a natural paradise where "white deer plough the fields, people ride on tigers, river deer are raised instead of dogs, pheasants sing in the morning, a person's bed is the soft green grass, bedcovers are the white clouds, curtains are the morning fog, and sun and moon are the only lamps. There are no restrictions on love, and youth lasts forever. There are no pain, no suffering, no tears and no sadness."

My Canadian friend, the photographer Ulli Steltzer, has come to Lijiang and Yongning four times, capturing many vivid images of Naxi and Mosuo people with her unique eye for artistic expression. From her pictures, I hope that people all around the world may have a taste of modern Naxi people's lovely timbre and happy countenance. When you have the time, please come to our beautiful "ancient kingdom." Come and make friends with the Naxi people

前　言

乌利·斯特尔兹

在过去6年里，我很荣幸能和云南的纳西人和摩梭人认识交往。当我1995年到达丽江时，一年前这儿发生了破坏性的地震，我既不会说汉语也不会说纳西话，只能用有限的手语交流。1997年、1999年、2001年，我再次来到丽江，也访问了永宁的摩梭村子以及中甸县的白地，在两位出色的翻译协助下，在我视觉印象的基础上，我对纳西人和摩梭人才有了更深刻的了解。

我们采访了许多人，这本书的图片文字，来自他们的言语和对世界的深刻理解。

这项工作，如果没有我们采访过和拍摄过的对象的好客和协作是办不到的，我对他们表示真诚的感谢。

我感谢和感激中国和加拿大的朋友们，我的这个计划得到了他们的大力支持。

云南社会科学院的杨福泉教授鼓励我，并且为这本书写了序言，作为一个丽江的纳西人，他慷慨地与我分享了他的纳西文化学识。

加拿大西门、弗雷泽大学（Simon Fraser University）王建（Jian Walls）教授，促使我出席了1999年在丽江召开的国际东巴文化学术讨论会。他总是乐于帮助我做一些翻译工作，包括将杨福泉教授为这本书所写的序译成英文。

1995年，在北京外国语学院工作的商惠民（Sandra Sachs）女士说服我去丽江，她在那儿从事关于"工合"的研究工作。1997年，我们返回那儿在一起工作。我深深地感激她，她为我提供的许多资料，为我的许多采访当翻译。谢谢你！亲爱的商惠民!(Sandra Sachs)

1999年，我将丽江东巴文化博物馆的赵秀云"借"出来两个星期，去摩梭人生活的永宁。她帮助我采访摩梭人，那些摩梭人和我一样地喜欢她。后来，她邀请我去参加她在白地举行的婚礼。

索纳米达娃（译音），Suonami Dawa那么和蔼，文雅！他与我们分享他的爱和摩梭人的传统知识，并且给我们介绍了永宁周围的许多家庭。

李锡，丽江县东巴文化博物馆馆长，他总是对人很关切，总是及时地提供我所需要的任何东西，包括翻译，运输车辆等。他待我像一个优秀的纳西人待他的母亲一样好。最后，我要谢谢非常热心的李忠翔教授，云南美术家协会的理事，对我的工作感兴趣并关注。并且介绍我认识云南美术出版社总编彭晓先生。

Vancouver　2001年5月

Foreword and Acknowledgements

by Ulli Steltzer

Over the past six years, it has been my privilege and joy to become aquainted with the Naxi and Mosuo people of Yunnan. When speaking neither Chinese nor Naxi, I arrived in Lijiang in 1995, the year before the devastating earthquake. Communication was limited to sign language. In 1997, 1999, and 2001, I returned and also travelled to the Mosuo villages of Yongning as well as to Baidi, in Zhongdian County. With the help of two exellent interpreters, I was able to add a considerable measure of understanding to my visual impressions. We interviewed the many people whose words and insights form the text of this book.

This work would have been impossible without the cooperation and hospitality of the people we interviewed and photographed. I offer them sincere thanks.

I am grateful and obliged to several friends in China and Canada who went out of their way to support this project:

Professor Yang Fuquan of the Academy of Social Sciences in Kunming encouraged me and provided the introduction to this book. A native of Lijiang, he generously shared his knowledge of the Naxi culture.

Professor Jan Walls, of Simon Fraser University made it possible for me to attend the 1999 Dongba Conference in Lijiang. Always willing to help, he made several translations for me, including Professor Yang Fuquan's introduction to this book.

Sandra Sachs of the Beijing Foreign Studies University persuaded me in 1995 to visit Lijiang, where she was involved with research on co-operatives. In 1997 we returned there to work together. I am indebted to her for much information and for translating many interviews. Thank you, dear Sandra!

Zhao Xiuyun is the translator for the Dongba Culture Museum in Lijiang. In 1999, I "borrowed" her for a two-week trip to Yongning's Mosuo people, who she interviewed and who loved her as much as I do. Later, she invited me to her wedding in Baidi.

Suonami Dawa, so kind and gentle! He shared with us his love and knowledge of Mosuo traditions and introduced us to many families in and around Yongning.

Li Xi, Director of the Dongba Culture Museum in Lijiang, always concerned, always aware, provided anything I needed, including interpreters and transportation. He treated me as a good Naxi treats his mother.

Finally, I thank the very kind Professor Li Zongxiang, Director of the China Artists Association, for his personal attention and interest in my work, and for introducing me to Peng Xiao, Chief Editor of the Yunnan Fine Arts Publishing House.

Vancouver, May, 2001

Contents: 目　录

Landscape and Architecture, Lijiang County 10-21　　丽江县的景观和建筑 10-21
Agriculture, Food Production and Marketing 22-35　　丽江县农业、食品生产和市场销售 22-35
Employment and Independent Work 36-51　　国营企业和个体户 36-51
The Young and the Old 52-65　　年轻人和老年人 52-65
Naxi Classical Music 66-75　　纳西古典音乐 66-75
Ritual and Celebration 76-87　　仪式和庆典 76-87
The Dongba Culture in Lijiang 88-93　　丽江县的东巴文化 88-93
The Dongba Cultue in Baidi, Zhongdian County 94-105　　中甸县白地的东巴文化 94-105
The Naxi and Mosuo people of Yongning, Ninglang County 106-141　　宁蒗县永宁的纳西人和摩梭人 106-141

Landscape and Architecture, Lijiang County

丽江县的景观和建筑

1. 生长在海拔 2400 米的棕榈树，背景是玉龙雪山和宏文村。
1. Palm trees at an altitude of 2400 meters; in the background is the Jade Dragon Snow Mountain, Hongwen Village.

2.流过丽江县的长江（金沙江）。
3.丽江县石鼓镇的金沙江支流。
2. The Yangtze River in Lijiang County
3. A tributary of the Yangtze River in the area of Shigu

4. 丽江古城。
5. 丽江古城里的古代石桥。
4. Lijiang Old Town
5. An ancient stone bridge in the Old
   Town

6. 在丽江的古城，汽车是不允许驶入的，甚至自行车也得推着走。
7. 走在丽江古城老街上的一个老妇人。
8. 玉湖村的"蜂窝岩"。
9. 白沙一户人家的庭院入口。

6. In Lijiang's Old Town, cars are not permitted, and even bicycles have to be pushed.
7. An old woman on an ancient street, Lijiang
8. The "beehive rocks" of Yuhu Village
9. The entrance to a courtyard, Baisha

8

9

10.丽江有多种多样的建筑风格。
11."起房子"（丽江）。

　　赭尚仁（译音，60岁）："这是我一生中第二次盖房子。我原来的房子在地震中遭到一些损坏，但这不是主要的问题，一条新开辟的路正巧要通过我原来的房子，所以，我得到这块地另建新房，我将和妻子、老父亲在这里生活。
　　像这样盖的房子，在地震中是不会倒塌的，因为它可以移动。建筑工人都是当地的。两小时以后，房子将起好，当房梁起好后，我要在'老年人协会'里请大家吃午饭。"

　　和社生（译音）："这是一座地地道道的纳西风格的房子。为起房子我们准备了3个星期，如果所有的工人和材料都能及时到位，在起房子之前，所有的砖瓦也都要准备好。在房子竖起来后，内部的装修需要长达五年之久的时间才能彻底完工。今年赭尚仁将搬进没完工的房子里去住，因为还有许多事情要做，没办法只能这样。"

10.Lijiang has a variety of building styles.
11. "House-Raising", Lijiang
　　Zhe Shangren, aged 60:

"This is the second time in my life that I am building a house. My last house was damaged during the earthquake, but that wasn't the main problem: It was in the path of the new road. So I was given this piece of land as a replacement. My wife and my old father will be living here with me. A house built like this won't fall down in an earthquake, because it can move. The construction workers are local. When the house-raising is finished, in about another two hours, I will invite everyone to lunch at the 'Old People's Association.'"

He Shesheng:

"This is an absolutely typical Naxi house. The preparation for the house-raising takes about three weeks if all the workmen and materials arrive on time. You have to have all the bricks in place as well, before you do the raising. But after that, it can take as long as five years until the house is completely finished on the inside. Zhe Shangren will move into his house within a year, but only because there is no alternative, and much will remain to be done."

11

13

12.石鼓镇的民居房顶。
13.丽江古城的民居房顶。
12. Rooftops of Shigu
13. Rooftops of Lijiang's Old Town

Agriculture, Food Production and Marketing
丽江县农业、食品生产和市场销售

14. 龙泉村的清晨。
14. Early mornig in Longquan

15. 王世顺（译音，宏文村）。
16. 奶牛的饲料（龙泉村）。
17. 一位准备去田间干活的老妇人（丽江县白沙乡龙泉村）。
18. 丽江古城附近的农耕。
15. Wang Shishun, Hongwen Village
16. Fodder for the cow, Longquan
17. An old woman ready to go to the field, Longquan
18. Farming near the Old Town

15

16

19

19.和发顺（译音，66岁）正在播种小麦（龙泉村）。
20.李玉芳（译音，丽江古城）。
　　李玉芳："我们全家都吃我种的菜，我不卖菜。"
19. He Fashun, aged 66, sowing wheat, Longquan
20. Li Yufang, Lijiang
　　Li Yufang:
　　" My family eats the vegetables　I grow.
　　I don't sell any."

21

22

21.洗干豆子（龙泉村）。
22.段秋月（译音，丽江古城）。
　　段秋月："从小我就种菜，并挑到市场上去卖。那时，这泉水清澈干净，里面有鱼，人们可以直接喝。现在的泉水很脏，连洗菜都不行了。"

21. Washing dried beans, Longquan
22. Duan Qiuyue, Lijiang
　　Duan Qiuyue:
　　"I grow vegetables and sell them in the market, I've done that from the time I was a child. At that time, the water was clear and clean. There were fish in it, and you could drink it. Now it is dirty. Now I shouldn't even wash vegetables in it."

29

23. 何漫月（译音，78 岁）正在市场上卖菜（丽江古城）。
24. 赵宗业（译音，85 岁）正在清理要拿到市场上卖的韭菜（丽江古城）。
25. 杨景乐（译音）在市场上一边照看她的曾孙子，一边卖瓜子。
23. He Manyue, aged 78, selling her vegetables in the market, Lijiang
24. Zao Zongye, aged 85, cleaning her green onions to sell in the market, Lijiang
25. Yang Jingle takes care of her great- grandson while selling sunflower seeds in the market, Lijiang

23

24

26. 陆秀珍（译音）正在打做豆腐的黄豆（丽江县白沙乡）。

    陆秀珍："我今年59岁，丈夫已经去世了，孩子们在丽江工作，他们请我到城里一起生活，但是，我拒绝了。因为我的身体还很好，什么事都能做，在自己家里我愿意做什么就做什么。我每天用黄豆和鸡豆做豆腐和凉粉，顾客都是本地人。"

27. 码垛（龙泉村）。

28. 和石生（译音）和周志跃（译音）与他们各自的孙子，他们正在做豆腐（丽江古城）。

26. Lu Xiuzhen, threshing yellow beans to make bean curd, Baisha

    Lu Xiuzhen:

    "I am 59 years old. My husband has already died. My children work in Lijiang; they invited me to come to the city to live with them, but I refused because I still have good health and can do what I like in my own house. I make bean curd every day, most buyers are local. I use yellow beans and chicken beans to make two kinds of bean curd.

27. Stacking rapeseed, Longquan

28. He Shi Sheng and Zhou Zhiyao with their respective grandchildren, making bean curd, Lijiang

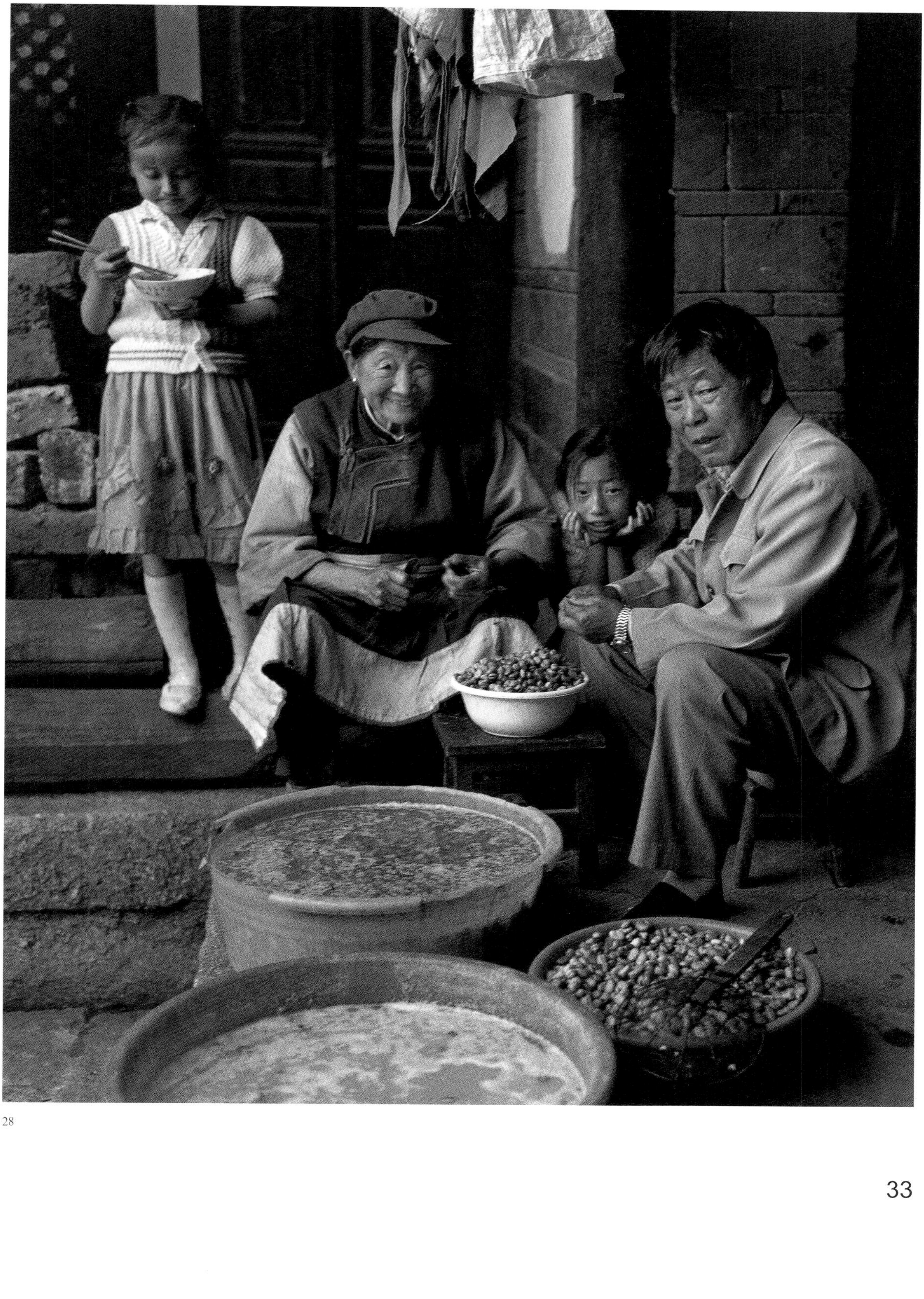

28

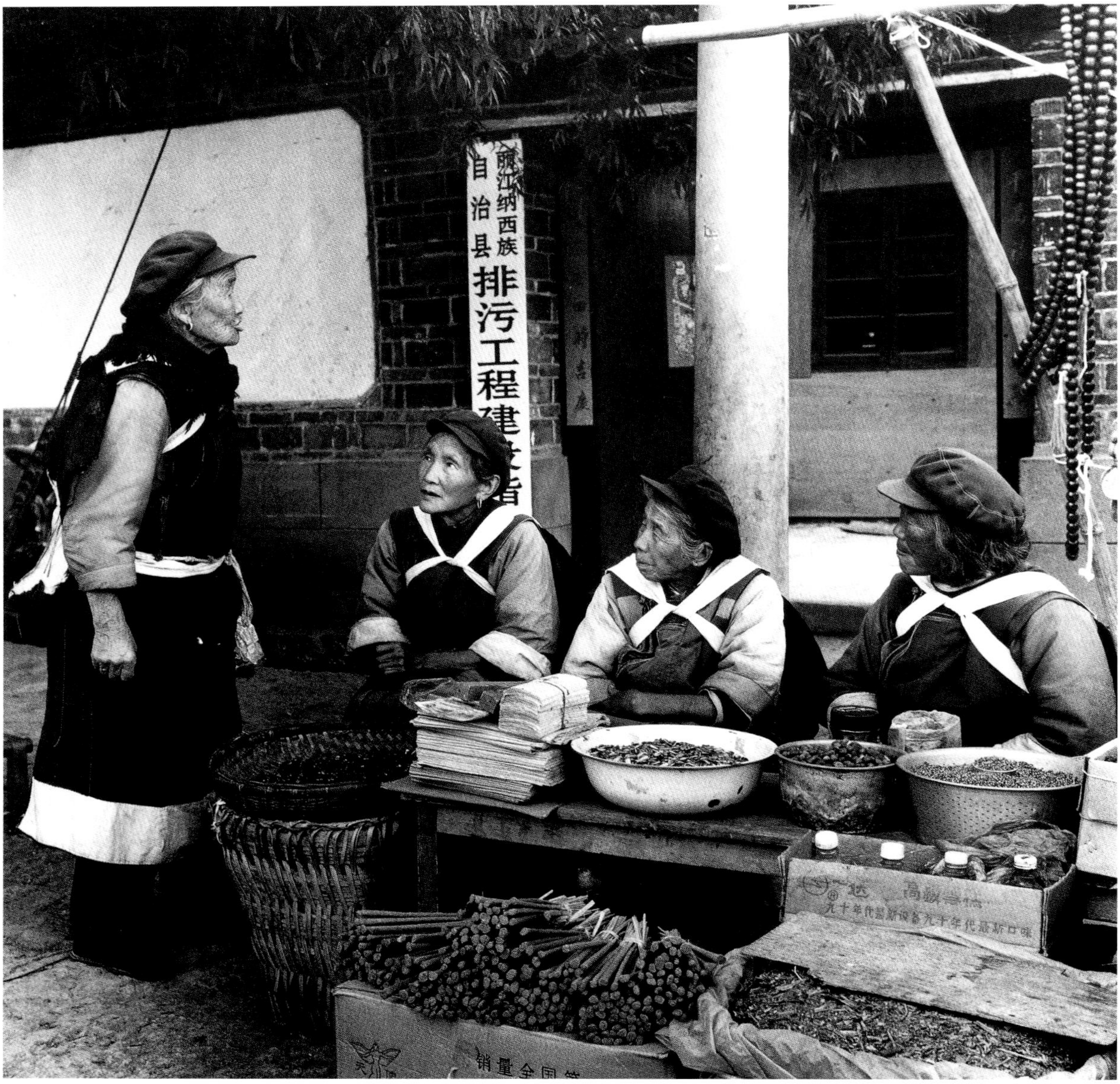

29

29. 在市场上聊天（丽江古城）。
30. 在一个卖小吃的热闹角落（丽江古城）。
31. 老城里的午饭时间。
29. Sharing news at the market, Lijiang
30. Snacks and treats at a busy corner, Lijiang
31. Lunch time in the Old Town

Employment and Independent Work

国营企业和个体户

32. 李桂兰（译音）和她的背带纺织机（龙泉村）。

李桂兰："我13岁时，妈妈就教我织布，我妈妈什么都会做，她把所有的本事都教给了我。

我在龙泉卖我编织的东西。按老习惯，女人有了孩子，她老婆婆应该送给她一个背孩子的背带，像我正在织的一样。因此这是人们需要的东西。但是，织一个很慢，纺麻纱就占去不少的时间。"

32. Li Guilan with her backstrap loom, Longquan

Li Guilan:

"My mother taught me to weave when I was thirteen. My mother could do anything and she taught it all to me. I sell my weavings to people in Longquan. When a woman has a baby, according to tradition, her mother-in-law must give her a baby carrier like the ones I weave. So people always want them, but weaving one is pretty slow, and spinning the wool also takes up a lot of time."

33. 玉龙村的一个农民正在编篮子。
34. 老城里一个理发店。
35. 龙泉村的裁缝王宗力（译音）和他的小孙子在一起。

33. A Farmer in Yulong Village weaving a basket
34. A beauty shop in the Old Town
35. Wang Zongli, tailor in Longquan, with his grandson

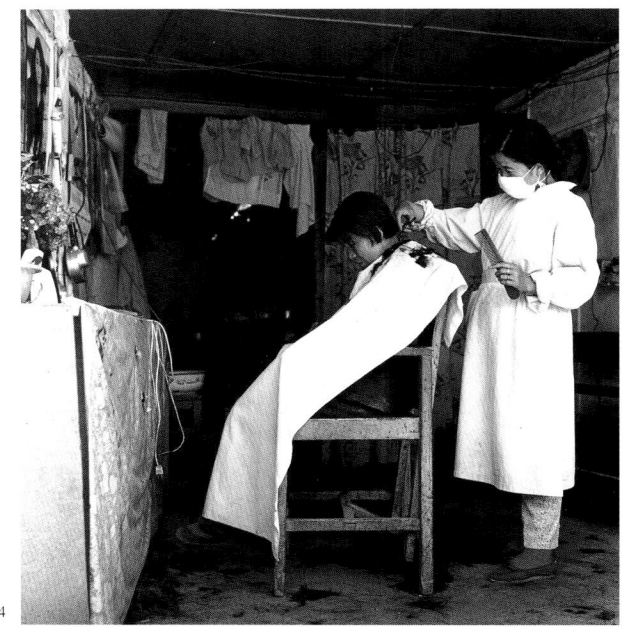

35

36

36. 和玉田（译音，丽江古城）。
　　和玉田："我们开这家店已经有20多年了。我们是个体经营，为顾客加工面条，三毛钱一斤。我们不让顾客使用机器，他们不知道怎样做，会把机器弄坏的。"
37. 小爱花（译音）在纺织厂纺线（丽江古城）。

36. He Yutian, Lijiang

　　He Yutian:

" We've been running this shop for more than twenty years. We are an individual enterprise. We process noodles for people. They bring the flour and we charge them 0.30RMB per jin (pound) to turn it into noodles. We don't let them use the machine themselves. They wouldn't know how. They might break it."

37. Xiao Aihua, spinning wool at the textile factory, Lijiang

38. 和集贤（译音）是顾彼德于1940年创立的"工业合作社"的一个"工合老人"。

　　和集贤："我相信什么呢？当我还是个孩子时，中国相当贫穷，我讨厌国民党。我曾在甘肃的山丹技术学校学习，我的老师是路易·艾黎（Rewi Alley）和国际工合的其它老师，'人人为我，我为人人'，'工合'是一个特别的组织，是致力于帮助穷人，使他们走出贫困线，解决基本的生活问题，然后走向富裕的一个特别的组织，这就是我相信的。"

39. 清洗李子（丽江食品加工厂）。

40. 在丽江鞋厂工作。

38. He Jixian, one of the "old co-operators" from Peter Goulart's co-operative of the 1940s

　　He Jixian:

　　"What do I believe in? When I was a child, China was desperately poor. I hated the Nationalist rulers of that time. At the Shan-Dan Training school in Gansu, I was taught by Rewi Alley and the people at the international Gung Ho. I was educated in 'All for one and one for all.' The co-op is an organization especially committed to helping the poor -- from poverty to subsistence to the beginnings of prosperity. That is what I believe in!"

39. Washing plums at the Lijiang Fruit Co-operative.

40. Work at the Lijiang Shoe Factory

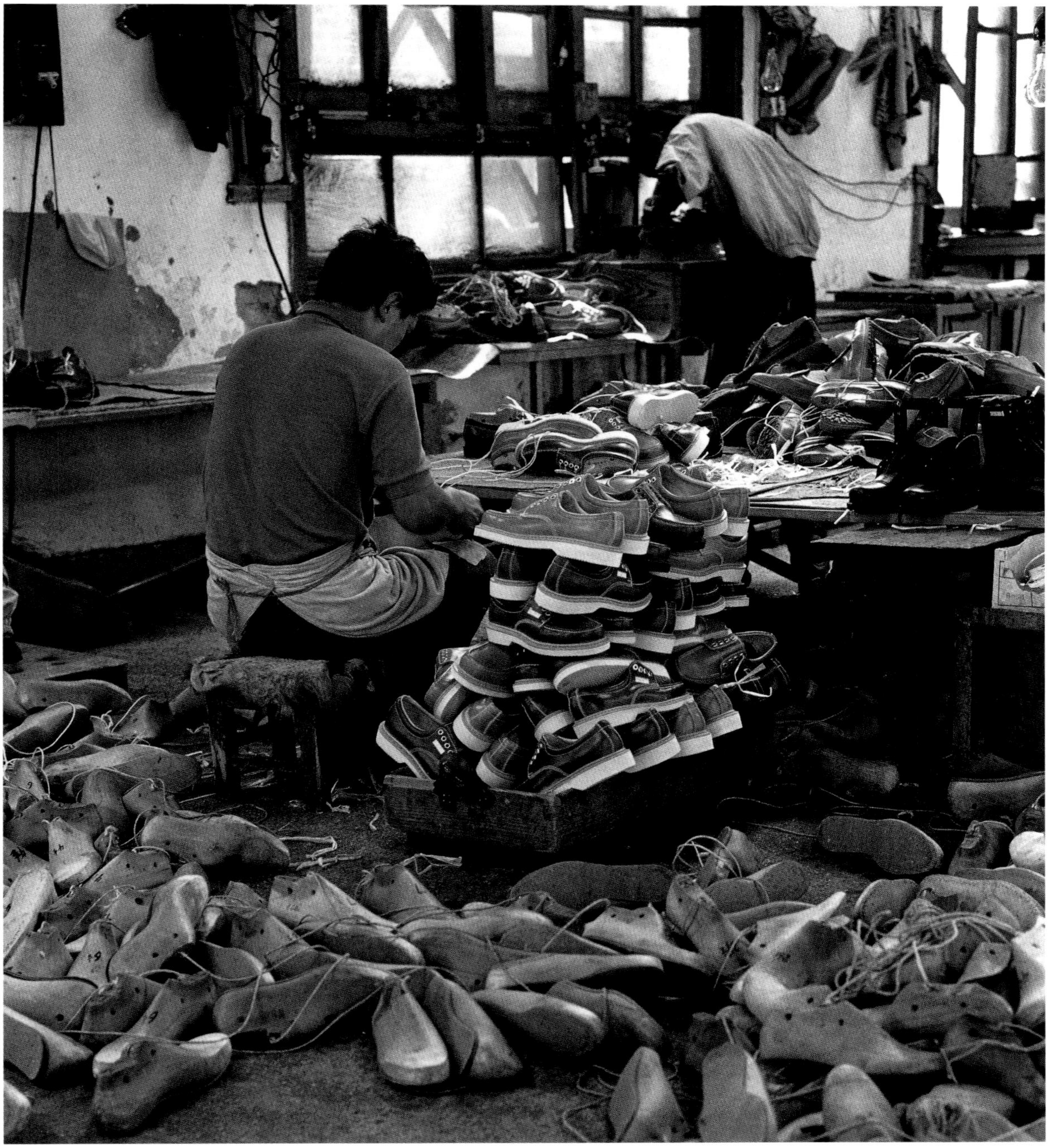

40

41. 李和林（译音）在黄山陶器厂后面他的花园里。

李和林："历史上，纳西人从未有过陶器，这是第一家陶器厂。自1961年起，我在这儿工作已经37年了，我是在这个厂成立后两年进厂工作的。刚建厂时我们只有20多个人，现在有74人了。最近，上海一家制陶厂与我们合作，帮助我们改进技术，所以，产量增加了。在这个时期（地震之后），我们开始生产盖房的瓦。现在不再做手工陶器。在市场上它们的售价不高，生产手工陶器很费时间，我们得不到相应的回报。在传统的龙窑里，产品损耗也太大。

同样，过去的生产方法需要用大量的木柴，而做瓦可以用煤。我们不是永远放弃了制作陶器，如果生产情况有好转，我们还会生产。尽管现在的条件不利，但是厂里每个人都很努力。如果整个企业的效益能提高，我们所有的人都会受益。

我的家和家人都在四川省的渡口，离这儿有270公里，因此，我单独生活，空闲的时间如果不种种花，很难度过每一天。我已经这样生活了28年，我未能经常与家人见面，一般是在一年一次的春节回去与他们团聚。"

42. 王秋芬（译音，68岁，丽江古城）。

王秋芬："1955年我开始在古城建立了做传统食品的妇女合作小食店，有些妇女做的面条、糕点、饼子、汤圆、豆沙等等很有名。我被选为合作社的经理。

开初，说服她们加入合作社小食店非常困难，古城里有名的厨师大都是妇女。她们都害怕失去自己的独立。1955年组织合作社，是政府的一项政策。

1957年政府也建立了国营饭店，它们与合作小食店不同。后来，有的合作社成员转到国营饭店去了，但不少的人仍然留了下来。

我们的薪水高低要看合作小食店每个月的收入情况。在家务事和经济方面，我们都互相支持，大家常常一起去公园玩。每年年底，合作社都给大家分一些红利。我们也可以向合作社借钱而不用付利息。

1980年，我们合作小食店买了一块地，盖了个旅社，一对年轻的店员夫妇管理这个旅社，旅社的收入用来发店员的退休金。现在搞市场经济，我们合作小食店经营有困难。由于经商的机会多了，很多人只想单独干，做个体经营者。"

41. Li Heling in his garden, behind the Huangshan Pottery

Li Heling:

"Historically, Naxi people never had a pottery. This was the first one. I have worked here for 37 years, since 1961, two years after it was started as a collective enterprise.

We were about twenty people when we began, now there are 74. A Shanghai ceramic factory has been working with us recently, to advise us on how to improve our technology, so our production has increased. At this time (after the earthquake), we have begun making roof tiles; we aren't making hand-crafted pottery any more - it didn't sell for a high enough price to justify the time it took to make. And there was too much breakage in the traditional dragon kiln. Also, our former production methods used too much wood. For tiles, we can use coal. We haven't permanently given up making pottery: We will return to it when we can. Conditions are not easy, but everyone is very hard-working. If we can improve the whole enterprise, we will all benefit. My home and my family is in Dukou, 270 km from here. So I live alone and in my spare time I grow flowers. If I didn't, I would have a hard time getting through the days. I have lived like that for 28 years. I don't get to see my family very often -- usually once a year at Spring Festival."

42. Wang Qiufen, aged 68, in Lijiang

Wang Qiufen:

"In 1955 I started the Women's Co-operative for Traditional Food in the Old Town. Some women were famous for their noodles, their cakes and dumplings, their black bean-curd, etc. I was elected to be their manager.

In the beginning, it was very difficult to persuade the people to be part of the organization. They were afraid to lose their independence. All the famous foodmakers were women. It was a policy of the Central Government in 1955 to work together.

In 1957 the government also established state-run enterprises. They were different from the co-operatives. So there were two systems. The older women stayed in the co-op, and all the young people had to be part of the State-owned restaurants.

Our salaries depend on the co-op's monthly income. We support each other in terms of family affairs and economics, and we try to enjoy ourselves once a month in the park. At the end of the year we get a share from the co-op. We can also borrow money from the co-op without interest.

In 1980 we bought a piece of land to build a hotel. It is managed by one couple. It provides money to help our older members when they retire. But now that the policies have changed, my work is very difficult because there are so many new businesses and so many people just want to work for themselves. They want to be private entrepreneurs."

43

43. 铜匠张自范（译音，83岁，丽江白沙乡）。

张自范："我爷爷和父亲都是很好的木匠。我14岁时，向本村的一位师父学会了做铜的手艺。有一段时间，我在国营企业里工作，退休后，我开了这个店。政府扶持我们，我连税都不用付。"

44. 皮匠张绍理（译音，龙泉村）。

张绍理："我13岁就学会了皮匠的手艺，1949年我参了军，1951年复员回乡后做农具。1970年我过金沙江去了中甸，为我们村赚钱。我做一些藏族喜欢的皮具，做装煤和粮食的皮口袋，为政府部门做皮椅子，为藏人做皮靴子。1980年以后，我才有能力独自开店自己经营。

100年前，我们村一些从事皮革业'杨'姓村民（也许还有其它姓）到永宁去经营，因为那边藏族多，买方市场很大。

1930年，在我们龙泉这儿已经有了皮革厂，后来搬到丽江去了。文化大革命时期，皮革厂停止生产皮革，开始做铜器。这就是为什么现在村里只有很少几个皮匠师傅的原因。我做皮革时用过各种各样的动物皮：牦牛、牛、猪、狐狸、豹子，还有猴子的，老虎皮只有在寺庙里才见得到。"

43. Zhang Zifan, aged 83, coppersmith, Baisha

Zhang Zifan:

"My grandfather and father were not coppersmiths, but they were very good at making wood furniture. I learned to be a coppersmith when I was fourteen years old from a person in my own village. For some years, I had a job working for the government, but I retired and opened this shop with the support of the government. I don't have to pay taxes."

44. Zhang Shali, leather craftsman, Longquan

Zhang Shali:

"I was thirteen years old when I learned leather work. But in 1949, I joined the army. When I came back, in 1951, I worked in the factory, making farmers' tools. Later, in 1970, I went to Zhongdian, across the Yangtze River, to earn some money for my village. I made leather bags for coal and grain, leather seats for the government and boots for the Tibetans. Only after 1980 was I able to work for myself.

About a hundred years ago, the 'Yang' family, and maybe a few others who all were leather craftsmen, moved to Yongning, because there was a great demand for Tibetan boots in that area. By 1930, a leather factory was opened here in Longquan; it was later moved to Lijiang. During the Cultural Revolution, the people there had to stop the leather work and work with copper. This is why there are only few leather craftsmen left.

I use all different kinds of leather: yak, cow, pig, deer, fox, leopard and monkey. Only in the temple do they use tiger skin."

44

45

45. 铁匠和工具匠和苏元（译音，72岁）（丽江县黄山乡白华村）。

和苏元："人们到这儿来请我做东西，原料由我提供，我是个体户。我的三儿子和我一起干活。我没有退休金。在乡下，我们老了只能依靠孩子们来抚养。"

（和苏元说，他是乡里手艺最好的铁匠。）

46. 银匠王哲新（译音，78岁）（丽江古城）。

王哲新："我是用铜和银做工艺品的，解放前，我做黄铜的门把手、门钉等，后来学会了做纳西、白族、彝族和其它少数民族喜爱的东西，比如说锁、锅、手饰、耳环、戒指、手链、给小孩的长命锁，挂在项链上的挂件等。

我工作的这个厂是地区一级的合作社，所用的材料全部是县里提供的。我们有5个人。根据当时的经济情况，有时我在当地的合作社工作，有时在县属企业工作，但无论在哪里，我做的工作都是一样的。

现在会银器制作技术的大多是老年人。退休后又到这儿来工作，因为我喜欢这个工作。"

45. He Shuyuan, aged 72, blacksmith and toolmaker, Baihua Village

He Shuyuan:

"People come and ask me to make things. I supply the material. I am a private entrepreneur. My third son works with me. I don't have a pension. In the countryside, we have to depend on our children when we get old ." (He Shuyuan is said to be able to make anything. He is the only person doing this work in the whole township.)

46. Wang Zhexin, aged 78, metal worker, Lijiang

Wang Zhexin:

"I work with silver and copper. Before Liberation, in the old society, I made brass locks. I learned to make objects prized by the Naxi, Bai, Yi and other minorities such as locks, hotpots and jewellery: rings, earrings, bracelets, and pendants in the form of a lock given to a child at birth to protect it.

This factory is a collective at the district level, so the county provides us with the metals we need. Five of us work here. According to the economic structure of the times, I was sometimes working in a collective, sometimes in a county enterprise - but the work was always the same.

Only the older people, for the most part, still know how to do these handicrafts. I came here after I retired so that I could keep doing what I was accustomed to doing and what I like doing."

46

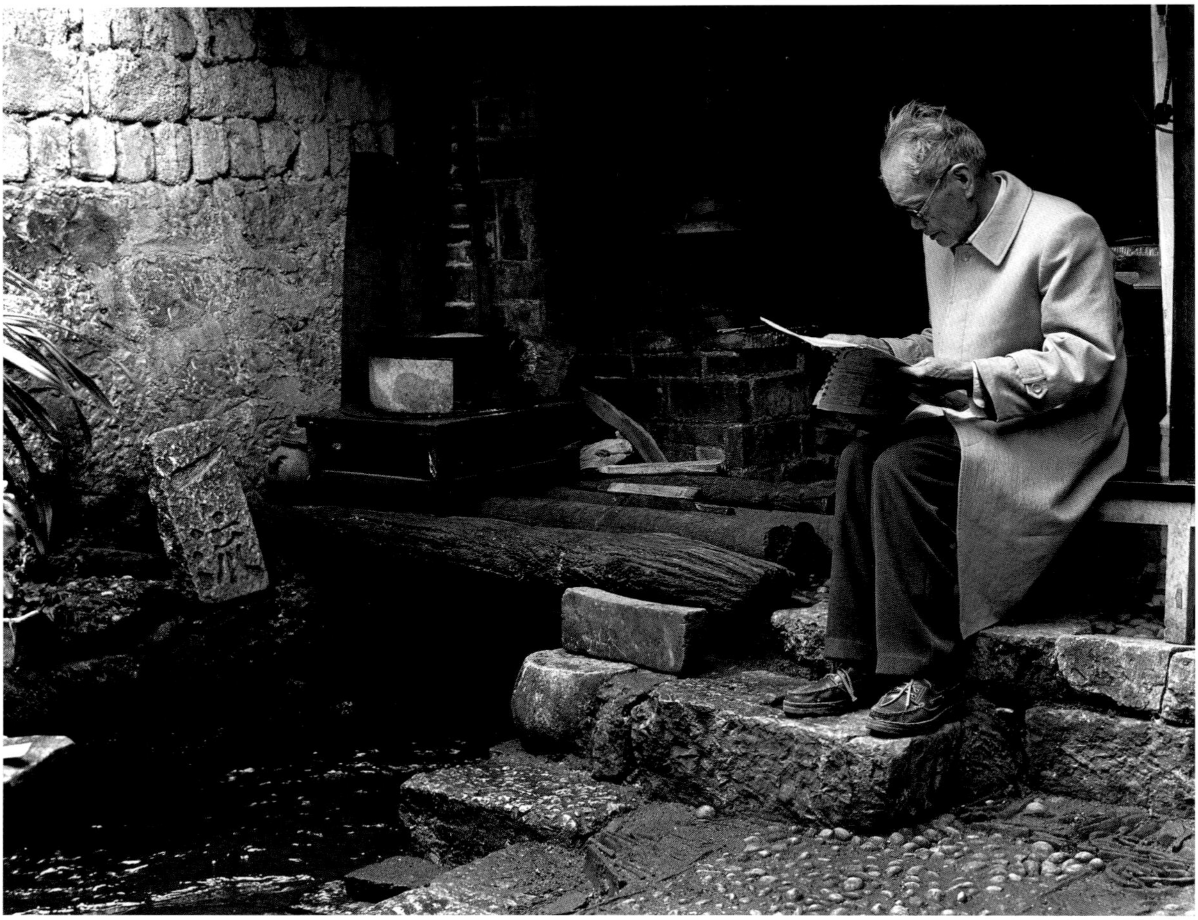

47

47. 赵和新（译音，丽江）。

赵和新："我是读书人的后代，祖上有人中过进士。我是做金银饰品的手艺人，木老爷（纳西土司）曾请我们去做过金银工艺饰品。这条巷是传统的打银器的地方，现在仍然叫'打银巷'，他们都是做银饰品的。石头上写着'一流'，泉水永不停歇地流过这个院子。这房子是明代的建筑（1368-1644）。"

48. 画家何万清在自己家里。

47. Zhao Hexin, Lijiang

Zhao Hexin:
"I am the offspring of intellectuals who passed the Imperial Examination 'Jinshi'. I am a craftsman of gold and silver. We were invited by the Naxi king to work with precious metal. This street is traditionally for craftsmen who work with silver, and still is called by that name. The stone you see says "The water flows"; the water has always been flowing through this courtyard. The house was originally built during the Ming Dynasty (1368-1644)."

48. Artist He Wanqing at his home

The Young and the Old
年轻人和老年人

49

49. 李功三，18岁，新闻小学的实习老师，(丽江。)

　　李功三："我认为孩子们能画一些来自真实生活的东西，这就是我为什么带他们出来到这儿的原因。

　　我毕业了，我决心到偏僻的村子教书，因为，我感觉那儿需要我，我的许多同学都有相同的感觉，我们决心到这样的地方去呆上几年。"

49. Li Gongsan, age eighteen, teacher in training,
　　Xingwen Primary School, Lijiang
　　Li Gongsan:
　　"I think it is good for the children to draw something from real life. That's why I brought them out here.
　　When I graduate, I am willing to teach at a remote village, because I feel I am needed there. Many of my classmates feel the same way. We are willing to stay in such a place for a few years."

50. 玉湖小学的教师李金南（译音）。
51. 小女孩（丽江古城）。
50. Teacher Li Jinnan at the Yuhu Elementary School
51. Little girl, Lijiang

51

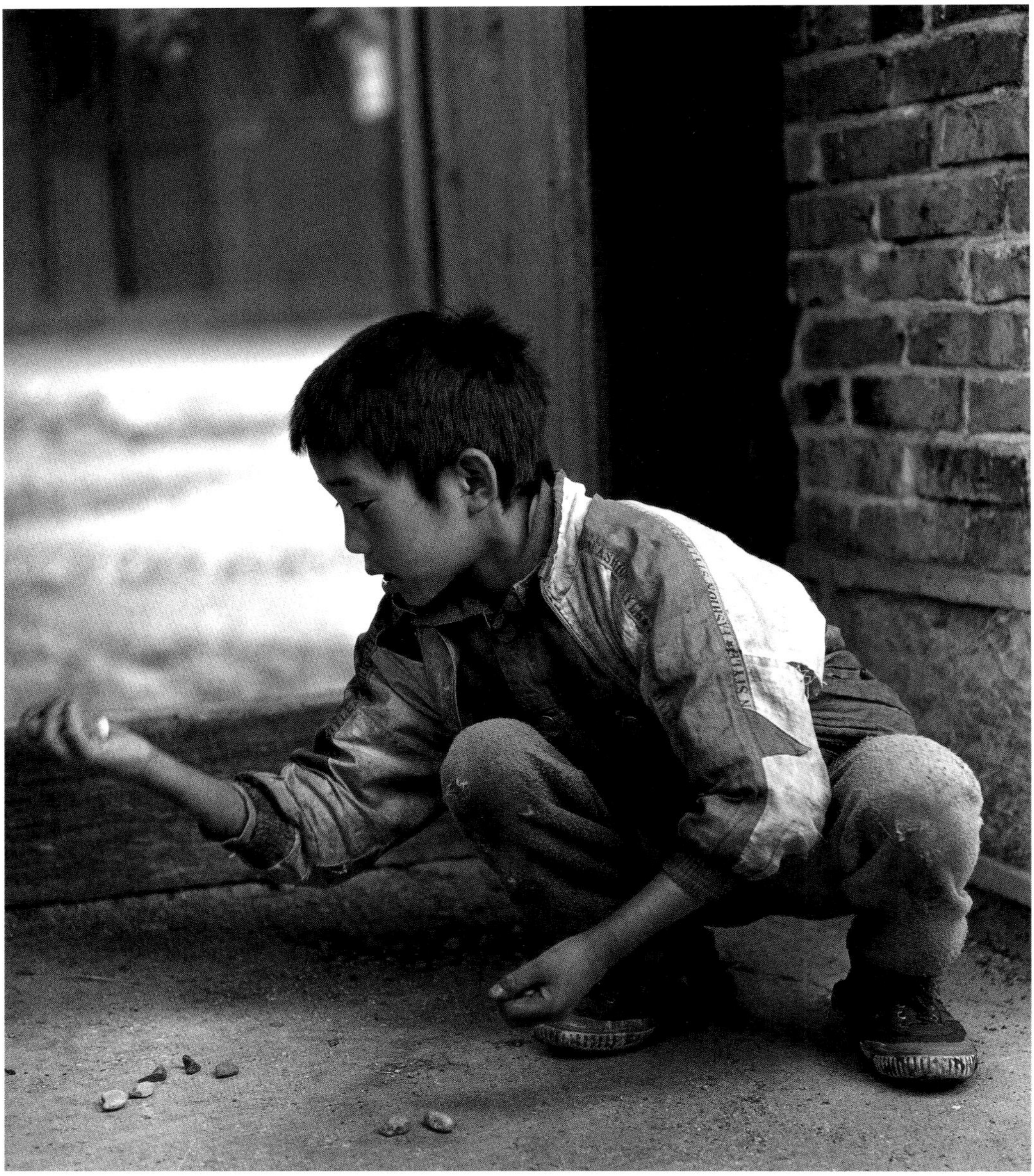

52

52. 孩子们在用鹅卵石玩一种古老的游戏（丽江县黄山乡白华村）。
53. 王丽梅（译音、14 岁）初中低年级学生（丽江古城）。

　　王丽梅："我们都认为将来要找一份好工作很难，所以大家现在都很用功。如果我有能力上大学，我想学理科，物理和数学是我所喜欢的两门课。

　　课外时间，男孩子喜欢踢足球，参加比赛。女孩子喜欢打篮球、唱歌跳舞。我喜欢读书，特别喜欢读的是科学杂志。"

52. Playing an ancient game with pebbles, Baihua village
53. Wang Limei, aged fourteen, junior middle school student, Lijiang

Wang Limei:

"We think good jobs will be hard to find, so we are all studying very hard right now. If I am able to go to university, I would like to study sciences, physics and maths; that is what I am interested in.

When we are not studying, the boys like to play football. They would love to take part in an international competition. The girls like basketball, singing and dancing. I like to read, especially science magazines."

54. 和然晓（译音，17岁），穿着母亲的传统服装，她结婚时将继承母亲的这套衣服（丽江古城）。

和然晓："我高中毕业，将要去北京上4年的大学，了解中国各个不同的民族。然后，我再回到丽江学习东巴文化和象形文字。

我现在必须学汉语、英语、数学、化学、生物和历史，所以没有时间学习东巴象形文字。在家里，我们说纳西话，但不是每个家庭都这样。有些年轻人认为汉语考试非常重要，在学校里他们彼此都说汉语，在家也这样。他们认为汉语和英语对赚钱和找工作都有好处。

我是个纳西女人，并且想为我的民族做点事情。我希望在将来什么时候，写一本关于纳西农民的书。我妈妈就是农民。"

55. 司瑞兰（译音）和杨贵雅（译音），购物归来在回家途中休息。

54. He Ran Xiao, aged seventeen, wearing her mother's traditional dress, which she will inherit when she gets married, Lijiang

He Ran Xiao:

"When I have finished high school, I will go to Beijing for four years to study the different Chinese nationalities at the university. Then I will come back to Lijiang to learn about the Dongba culture and pictographs.

Now I have to study Chinese, English, maths, chemistry, biology and history. So there is no time to study the Dongba pictographs. I think, the school should teach the Naxi language, too, but the teachers and the government don't think so. At home, we speak Naxi, but not every family does that. Some young people think that the Chinese exam is so important that they only speak Chinese with each other in school and also at home. They think that both Chinese and English, are good for finding jobs and making money. That may be so, but it is very dangerous for the Naxi culture in the future.

I am a Naxi woman and want to do something for my people. At some time I hope to write a book about the Naxi farmer. My mother is a Naxi farmer."

55. Si Ruilan and Yang Guiya, resting on their way home from shopping

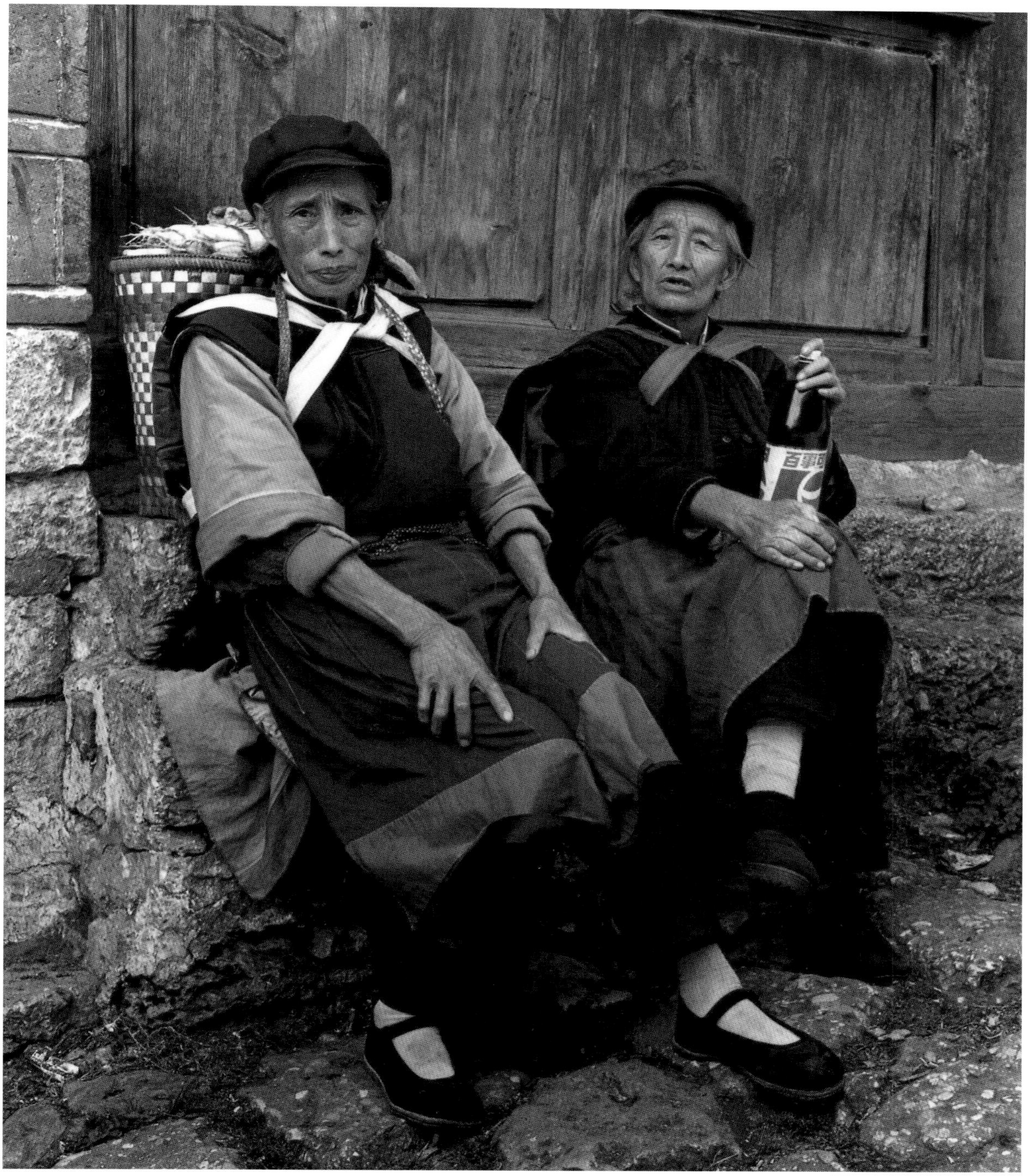

55

56. 和华庚（译音，88 岁，丽江古城）。

和华庚："我常常喝酥油茶、吃凉粉这些简单的食物，用蜂蜜和猪胰子做的肥皂洗澡，用盐刷牙，这是传统方法。我不用年轻人用的化学的东西，它们对身体并不好。

我 27 岁就守了寡。我不想再婚。即便我是出身在一个富裕的家庭，我也像一个普通人一样地劳动，抚养我儿子和 3 个孙子，我赚生活所必需的钱。我儿子现在已经 60 多岁了。

家人们想让我把烟戒掉，但是我每天只抽一支。"

57. 和玉高（译音，73 岁）在溜鸟（丽江古城）。

和路（译音，和玉高的儿子）："我父亲过去是丽江地区中学的教师。文化大革命期间，他被打成了'反革命'，下放到一所小学教书。那时他失去了党籍。1979 年，邓小平恢复工作后，我父亲的党籍也得到了恢复。1983 年我父亲退休了。现在，他喜欢在院子里养鸟种花，每天早晨跑步 6-7 公里，还做早操。"

58. 何玉高（译音）的妻子张自茹（译音，72 岁），在他们家的院子里。

张自茹："我用皮带栓着猫，是因为她喜欢去惊扰我丈夫的鸟。"

56. He Huageng, aged 88, Lijiang

He Huageng:

"I usually take yak butter tea and black beans, simple food, and I wash myself with honey and pig soap. I use salt to clean my teeth, the traditional things, not the chemical things young people use, they are not good for you and take away your living colour.

When I was 27 I became a widow. I did not want to get married again, and even though I come from a rich family, I worked as a labourer to raise my son, and later three grandchildren, to make the money we needed. My son is more than 60 years old now.

My family tries to stop me from smoking, but I only smoke one cigarette a day."

57. He Yugao, aged 73, walking his birds, Lijiang

He Lu, son of He Yugao:

"My father used to be a teacher a the District Middle School. During the Cultural Revolution, he was sent to the countryside to teach in a primary school. He was accused of being a counter-revolutionary Nationalist supporter. He lost his Party membership as well at that time. Deng Xiaoping rehabilitated him in 1979, and in 1983 my father retired. Now he likes to raise birds and look after the flowers in the courtyard. He grew them all. Every morning he goes running 6 to 7 km and he does morning exercises, too."

72. Zhang Ziru, aged 72, wife of He Yugao, in their courtyard

Zhang Ziru:

"I keep the cat on the leash because she likes to bother my husband's birds."

59. 木仁（译音，75岁）和自别（译音，64岁），孙子们的保姆（龙泉村）。
60. 和实军（译音）。
    和实军"我一直照顾我的两个孙子。退休前，我是白沙小学的教师，我教1-4年级，我总是喜欢那些小一点儿的孩子们。"
61. 散步（龙泉村）。
62. 一位老妇人背着沉重的口袋（丽江古城）。

59. Mu Ren, aged 75, and He Zibie, aged 64, babysitting their grandchildren. Longquan
60. He Shijun:
    "I still look after both my grandchildren. Before I retired, I was a teacher at the Baisha Primary School. I taught grades one to four, and I have always loved those little ones."
61. Going for a walk, Longquan
62. An old woman carrying a heavy load, Lijiang Old Town

61

62

63. 白沙村附近佛教寺庙的看门人。

64. 正在家里打牌的杨春仙(译音，丽江古城)。

杨春仙："我们家奶奶87岁了。另外的女人是我们的邻居，她们都退休了，年龄都在70–80岁之间。她们来这儿玩牌，因为，孙子们都长大了，好长时间了，她们没有多少事情可做。有时她们也玩麻将，但从来不赌钱。"

65. 老人们（丽江古城）。

杨静(译音)："你从来说不清那些男人们会在哪儿，也许他们告诉妻子们，出去几分钟，但是如果遇到一个朋友，他能去一整天。如果妻子要求他们做点家务事，他们只帮着照看一下孙子。退休的女人们有很多家务事要做，比如去集市买东西、做饭、照看孩子，退休的男人们则没有多少责任。"

63. The keeper of the Buddhist temple near Baisha

64. Playing cards at the home of Yang Chunxian, Lijiang

Yang Chunxian:

"Our grandmother is 87 years old. The other women are neighbours, they are all between 70 and 80 and retired. They come here to play cards because their grandchildren are grown up and have been for a long time. They don't have anything to do. Sometimes they play Mahjong, but they never play for money."

65. Old men, Lijiang

Yang Jing:

"You can never tell where the old men will be. They may tell their wives they are going out for a few minutes, but if they meet a friend, they can be gone all day. They only look after their grandchildren if their wives ask them to. But she would have to ask. Retired women still have responsibilities: to shop in the market, cook, look after children. Retired men have no responsibilities."

65

Naxi Classical Music
纳西古典音乐

66. 木实青（译音，78岁）（丽江县黄山乡白华村）。

木实青："我从来就不是乐队成员。过去，演奏古乐是地主和生活条件好的人，几乎没有普通老百姓会演奏的。

我年轻时，做梦也想不到会有现在这样的房子。我在这个院子里出生和长大，家里包括我已有八代人在这里生活过。我的孙子是第十代。我们是木氏家族的成员，祖先是从白沙来的。我年轻时，这个院子只建好了一边。我的父母只说纳西话。那个时候粮食产量很低，没有肥料。"

木为（译音，木实青的儿子）："我父亲的家庭非常穷，他的父母为他进学校作出很大的牺牲。高中毕业，他为了逃兵役到了大理，后来当了老师。那个时候，所有的老百姓都赤着脚，他们从来没有见过鞋子。"

66. Mu Shiqin, aged 78, Baihua village

Mu Shiqin:

"I have never been a member of the music group. The old music was played by those whose conditions were good, landlords and people like that. Very few ordinary people played. When I was young, we could not have dreamed of having a house like we have now. I was born and grew up in this courtyard, and eight generations of my family, including me, have lived here. My grandson is the tenth generation. We are members of the Mu clan and originally from Baisha. But when I was young, only one side of the courtyard was built. My parents spoke only Naxi. Grain yields were very low. In their days there was no fertilizer."

Mu Wei, son of Mu Shiqin:

"My father's family was very poor, but his parents sacrificed a lot to see that he went to school. He graduated from high school and went to Dali to escape having to join the army and became a teacher. At that time all common people were barefoot. They didn't ever see shoes."

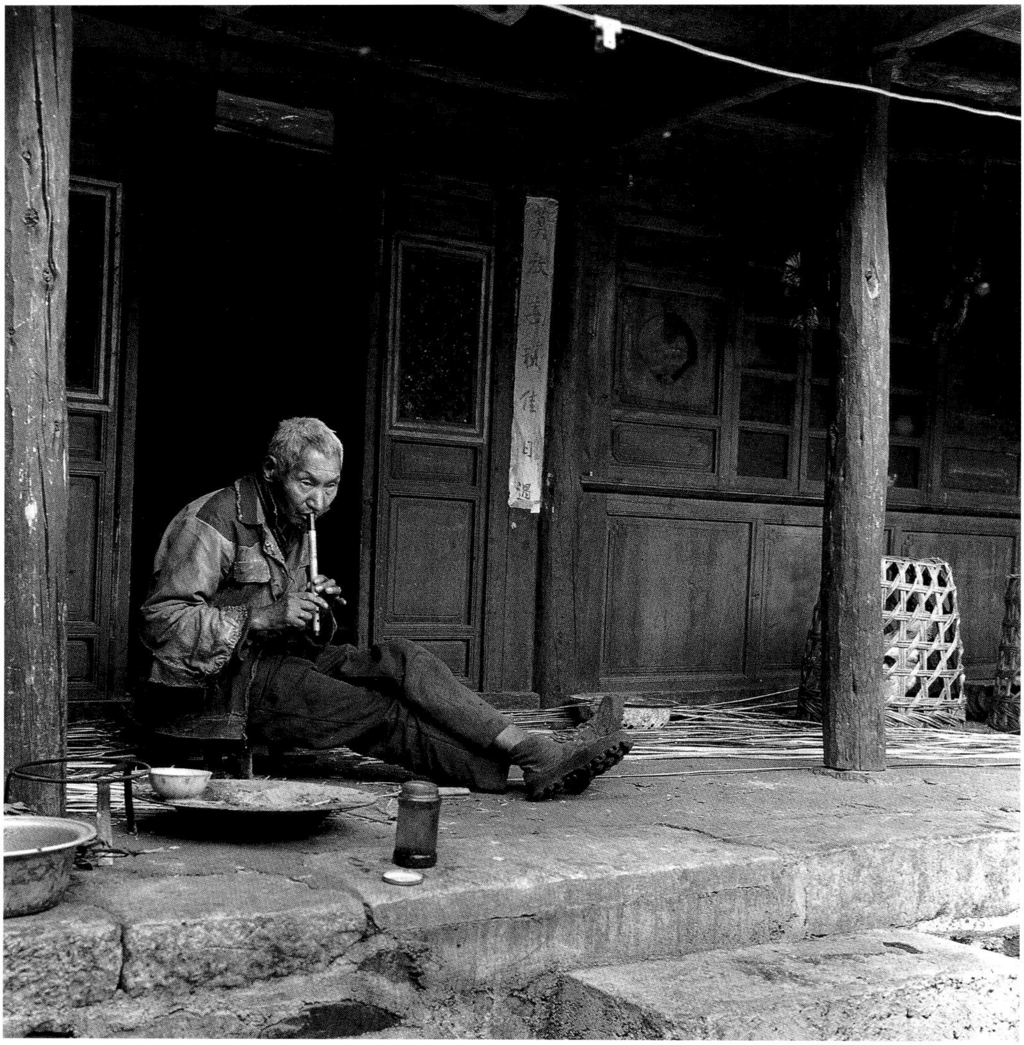

67

67. 一个农民在家门口吹笛子(丽江县黄山乡白华村)。
68. 木为元（译音）正走在参加朋友们的"纳西古乐队"活动的路上（白华村）。

    星期六，这些人聚在一起，为自己的兴趣而演奏。他们演奏传统的纳西音乐，这种音乐几乎都是小调。这个乐队的乐师们大多数都能演奏一种以上的乐器。
69. 和国为（译音），正在演奏二胡，背景中敲打击乐的是木为元。

67. A farmer playing the flute at his home, Baihua Village
68. Mu Weiyuan, on his way to join his fellow musicians of the Naxi Classical Music Troupe, Baihua Village

    These people come together on Sundays to play for their own enjoyment. They play the traditional Naxi music, which is always in a minor key. Most of the participants in this group are able to play more than one instrument.
69. He Guowei, playing a two - string instrument, in the background Mu Weiyuan with bells

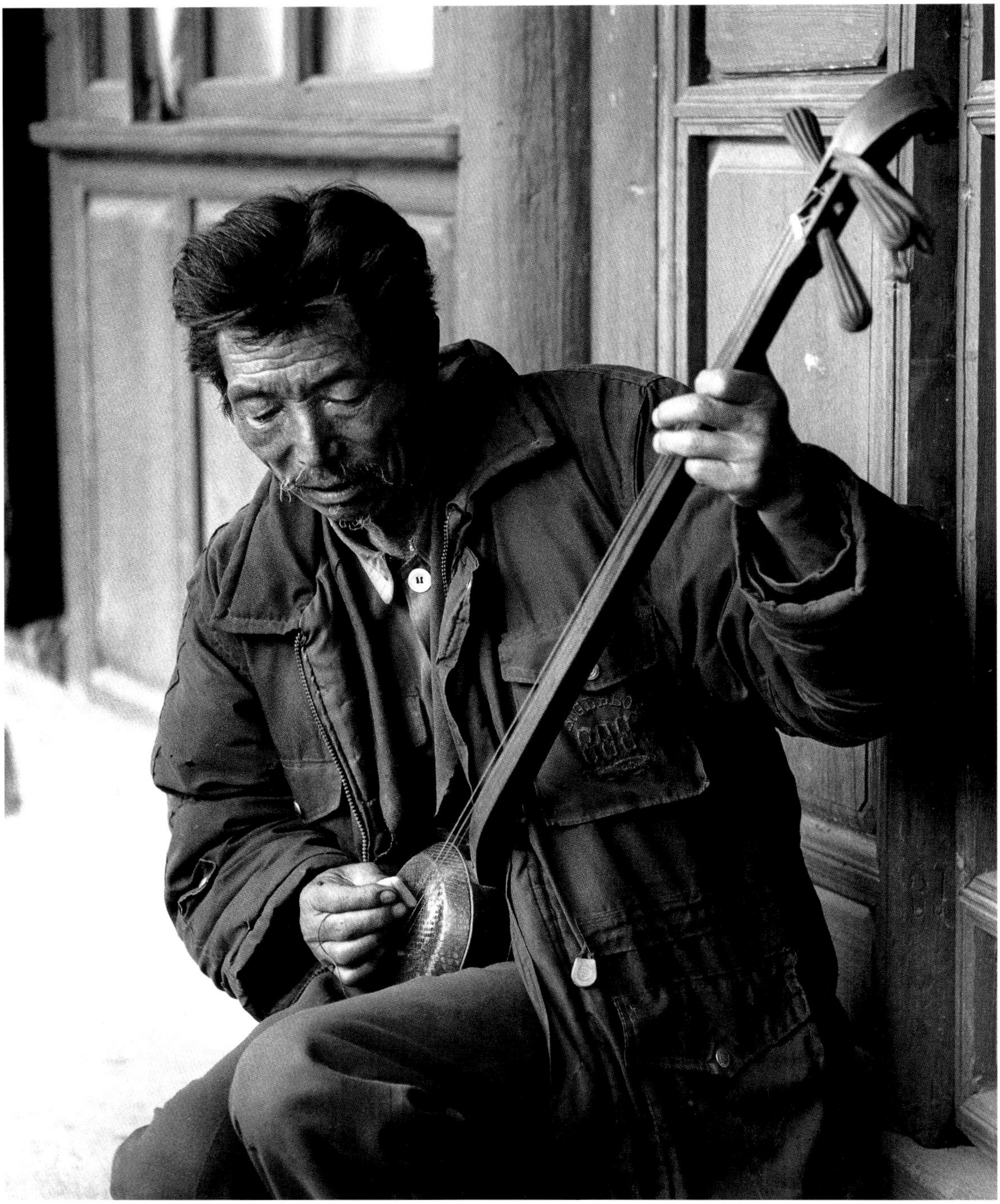

70

70.和学胜（译音）和其它乐队成员。
71.纳西古乐队。

70. He Xuesheng, another member of the group
71. The Naxi Classical Music Troupe

72. 黄山村纳西乐队的两个队员（两张图片）。
73. 黄山村纳西乐队。
72. Members of the Huangshan Village Naxi Music Group (two photos)
73. The Huangshan Village Naxi Music Group

73

74. 宣科—丽江大研纳西古乐会指挥。

宣科："演奏音乐提高了一些本地老人的地位。只有这些人才会演奏，他们从前是地主，出生在旧社会的普通的老人是不会玩乐器的，从前，地主是被人看不起的。

赵鹤年是位商人。他从鹤庆、剑川旅行到丽江，买了再卖。在抗日战争期间，他碰到了机遇使生意获得成功。他带领的商队有六七十人，一百匹牲口，并且与印度人做贸易。因此，他必须使自己成为一个非常强壮、聪明无畏的人，一个无论在任何情况下都有能力的人，一个能够统帅其他人的人。他就是那种可以领导一队马帮的有这么一种能力的人。他会说藏语，为了自己的商业目标，他必须懂藏语。他儿子是中医院的一位很好的草药医生。

习家驹出身于贵族家庭，他父亲是国民党将军，因为家庭的原因，他受过很好的教育。1949 年，28 岁他结婚时，他们的那桩婚姻在丽江众人皆知。他妻子是最漂亮的纳西女人之一。他出身于最有钱的四个大家庭中的一个。"

75. 赵鹤年（译音，84 岁）和习家驹（译音，76 岁），丽江大研纳西古乐会成员。

74. Xuan Ke, director of the Classical Music Academy in Lijiang

Xuan Ke:

"Performing the music has raised the status of some of the local old people. The only people who could play it were former landlords; old people who were ordinary people in the old society didn't know how to play it. And former landlords were people who had been looked down on in recent years.

Zhao Henian was a businessman, He travelled from He Qing and Jianquan to Lijiang, buying and selling. But his great opportunity came along during the war years. He led a caravan of 60 to70 men, a hundred animals, and became involved in the trade with India. So he had to be very strong and very wise, a courageous man, a man able to take what the weather could do, a man who could command other men. He was the sort of person who could lead this caravan. He could speak Tibetan, because he had to know it for business purposes. His son is a good herbal medicine doctor at the Chinese Medicine Hospital.

Xi Jiaju's family was a 'royal' family. His father was a famous Nationalist general. He was very well educated because of the family's position. In 1949, at the age of 28, he got married. That marriage is famous in Lijiang. His wife was one of the most beautiful of Naxi women. He came from one of the four families with the most money: his uncle was a district commander. So, unfortunately, in that same year, his whole family was sent for re-education, and they all became labourers. All of us went for 21 years to prison, until 1978, when they reversed the verdicts. We all asked to return home. We all came back. Once a prisoner, now a hero."

75. Zhao Henian, aged 84, and Xi Jiaju aged 76, members of the Naxi Ancient Music Academy in Lijiang

75

Ritual and Celebration
仪式和庆典

76. 李红月（译音）和赵淑平（译音）。

赵淑平："我们俩都在旅游局工作。我是汉族,但被纳西人收养了。我丈夫是纳西人,他是一所中等技术学校的负责人。

在旅游局大家对我都很好。很多同事都是同学。在各级政府部门里,男人当领导的多,但公务员有一定的比率必须是女的。

汉族男人和纳西男人对待女人有较大的差别。汉族男人容易与家庭和睦相处,听妻子和母亲的。而不少纳西男人只关心他们认为是'重要的事',而把所有的家务事都留给妻子,这是一种传统习俗。但在另一方面,纳西男人很善于表达自己的情感。"

76. Li Hongyue and Zhao Shuping

Zhao Shuping:

"We both work for the Tourist Bureau. I was born Han - Chinese, but I am Naxi by adoption. My husband is also Naxi. He is the principal of the Technical Middle School. In the Tourist Bureau the men treat me well. We were all classmates when we were students. But it is true that, at all levels, men are in the leading positions. There is a ratio; a certain number of officials must be women. Han - Chinese and Naxi men differ quite a bit in their treatment of women. Han - Chinese men are easier to get along with in family relationships. A Han - Chinese man will listen to his wife and to his mother. For the Naxi man. it is a tradition to concern himself only with 'important business' and leave all the household chores and so on to the woman. But on the other hand, Naxi men are very good about expressing feelings and emotions."

77. 和永中（译音）和他的妻子赵谢志（译音，丽江县白沙乡龙泉村）。

和永中："在旧社会，你的婚姻是无法自己选择的。媒人在纳西人中还存在，我们是通过一位家庭成员介绍而认识的。

我父亲是丽江九河人，是个木匠，现在住在龙泉村。我妻子的父亲也是九河人。父亲希望我找一个九河姑娘结婚，这样，我就永远有回家的理由。所以，我们是这样相识的，1983年结的婚。"

78. 在王玉玉（译音）和杨永明（译音）的婚礼上，所有的贺礼都很细致地登记在册。

79. 举行婚礼那天，和进阙（译音）背着新娘子齐思英（译音）走进他们家的院子，客人们跟随在后。

77. He Yongzhong and his wife, Zhao Xiezhi, Longquan
He Yongzhong:

"In the old society, there was no choice about who you married. When we met, the Naxi still used matchmakers, but we were introduced through a family member. My father came from Jiuhe. He was a carpenter and worked in Longquan. My wife's father also came from Jiuhe. When it was time for me to get married, my father wanted me to marry someone from Jiuhe, so that I would always have a reason to come home. So we were introduced. We got married in 1983."

78. At the wedding of Wang Yuyu and Yang Yongmen, all gifts are meticulously registered.

79. On their wedding day, He Jinque carries his bride, Qi Siyin, into his family's courtyard. The guests follow them inside.

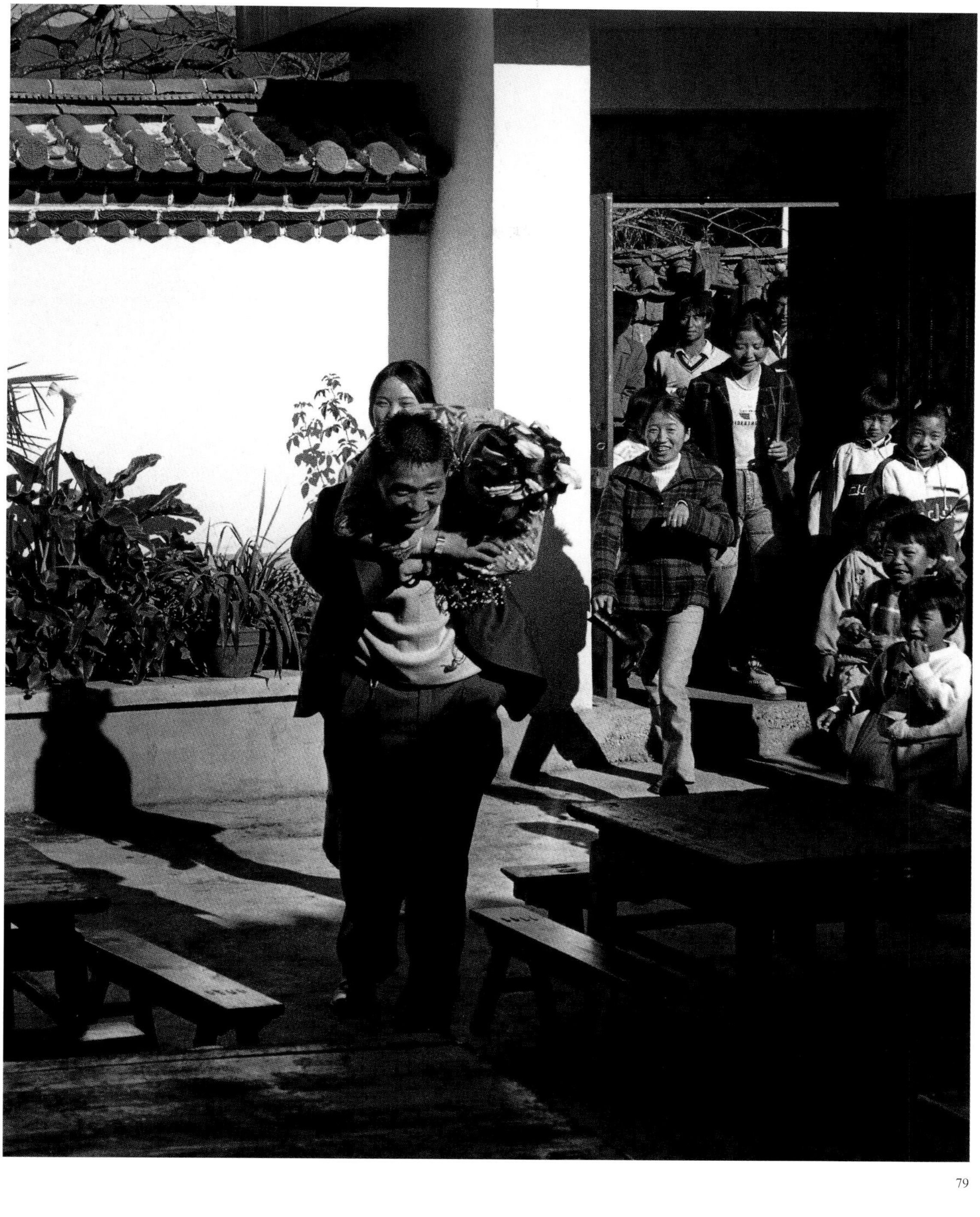

80. 新郎背新娘入洞房。

赵秀云（译音，24岁，博物馆职工）："我自己是纳西人。我认为年轻的纳西妇女不喜欢穿传统的纳西服装，她们宁愿穿现代的、时髦的服装。因为传统的衣服很笨重，不方便。按老习惯，每一个纳西女孩子都要有一套合身的传统服装，那是她和她的女性亲属为她做的嫁妆。现在，对大多数妇女来说，这似乎有点陈旧了。"

81. 一对年轻的新婚夫妇。

82. 参加婚礼的客人们在院子里的筵席上。

杨静（译音）："吉利的日子是每个月里的双数，如果阴历、阳历都是双数是最佳的日子。这就是为什么人们要在冬天的双月结婚的部分原因。另一个原因是有冰箱的家庭很少，即使有冰箱也不够大，他们害怕婚宴上的食物变质。"

80. The groom carries the bride into the house

Zhao Xiuyun, aged 24, museum staff:

"I am a Naxi myself. I think young Naxi women don't like wearing the traditional Naxi dress. They would rather wear modern, stylish clothing, because Naxi clothing is heavy and clumsy; it isn't convenient. It used to be that every Naxi girl had a special set of traditional clothing which she and her female relatives made for her wedding. Now, for most young women, even this seems to be a thing of the past."

81. Qi Siyin and He Jinque, the happy young couple

82. Wedding guests at the feast in thecourtyard

Yang Jing:

"Auspicious days are double digit days and months. It is best of all if they are double on both the Lunar and the Roman calendar. This is partly why people get married in winter - the double digit months. The other reason is that few people have refrigerators or, if they have them, they are small - and they are afraid the food for the wedding banquet will spoil."

82

83. 杨学连（译音，72岁）的葬礼（丽江县白沙乡玉龙村）。
    妇女们匍匐在棺木前，另一些村民带着礼物、大米、玉米和面粉等进入他家的院子。

84. 送葬时，离开院子后，妇女们首先沿着山丘向三多（三多是纳西人的保护神）庙方向走去。她们排成一行趴在地上，男人们抬着棺木从上面越过，这象征"通向另一个世界的桥"。妇女是不允许跟随男人们到墓穴去的，她们只能在后面表示哀悼。

83. At the funeral of Yang Xueliang, aged 72, in Yulong Village, women bow down to the coffin while others bring presents of rice, corn and wheat into the family's courtyard.

84. Leaving the courtyard first, the women walk up the hill towards the Sanduo Temple. They line up on the ground in a long row, and the men carry the coffin over the "Bridge to the other world". Not permitted to follow the men to the gravesite, the women stay behind, languishing in their grief.

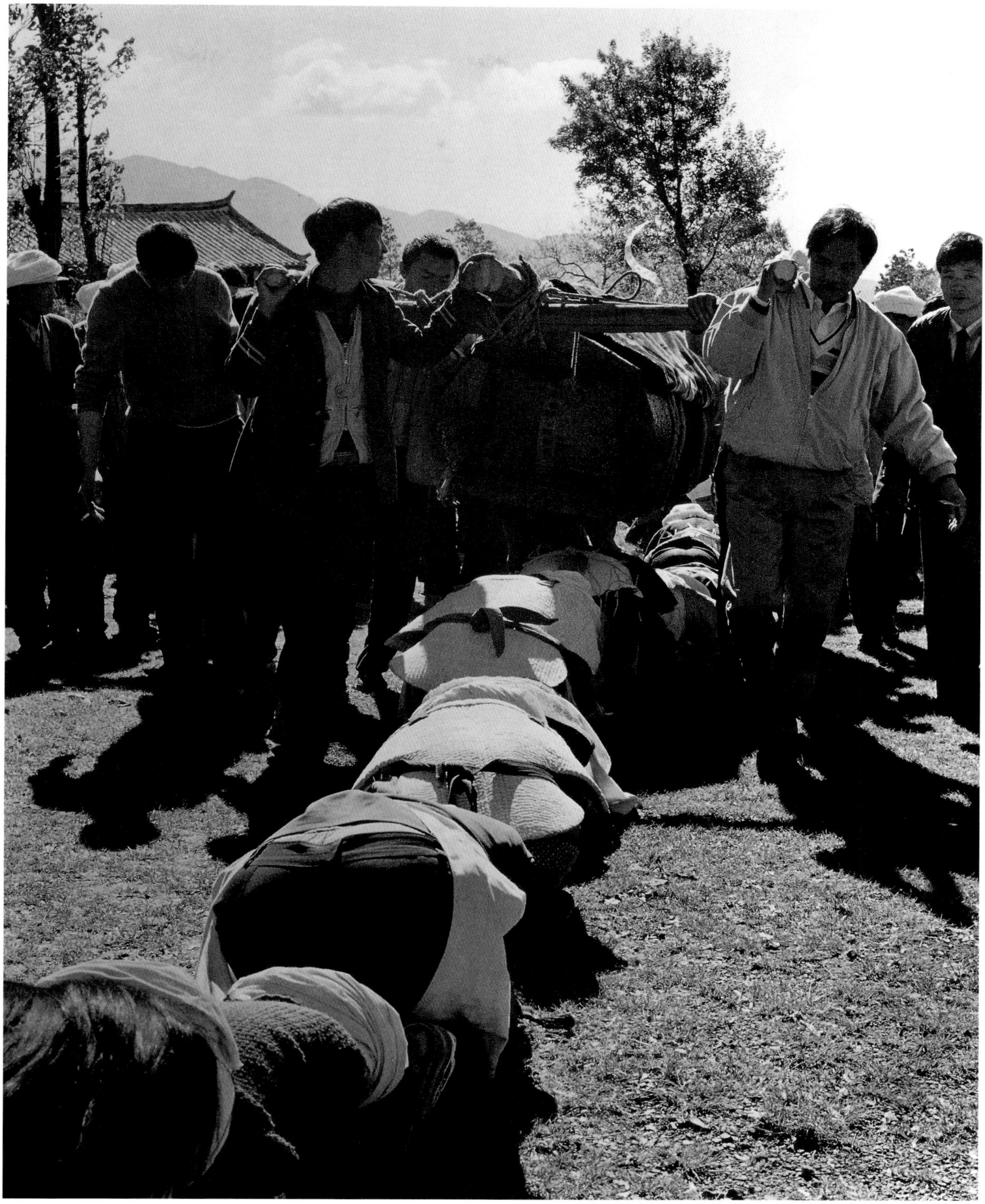

84

85. 丽江古城附近的一个墓地。
86. 每年清明节那天，家庭成员们都要到他们祖先的坟地扫墓。
87. 李奇红（译音）为婆婆和爱合（译音）的坟墓带去新鲜的树枝。

和刚力（译音，李奇红的丈夫）："所有的坟墓都有漂亮的墓碑，但是，在文化大革命期间，墓碑被看作是'四旧'。所以，人们把它们都拆了。

现在，人们开始重新修坟，大家都修得起。有好几代人都葬在这儿。有些坟墓有几百年了。我们家在解放前就买了这块地，我爷爷就葬在这儿。这是我妈妈的坟，她是1984年去世的。

有一个时期是不准跳舞的，现在又流行起来了。一年中大家到墓地来两次，另一个时间是春节大年初一或初二，那时他们不是专门来扫墓的，只是来游览游览。"

85. A gravesite near Lijiang
86. Every year, on the the Day of the Dead, the "Qing Ming Festival", family members clean and decorate their ancesters' graves.
87. Li Qihong brings fresh branches to the grave of He Aihe, her mother-in-law.

He Gangli, husband of Li Qihong:

"All these graves had beautiful stones, but during the Cultural Revolution, gravestones were considered part of the 'Four Olds' and the peasants took them away. Now, as people can afford it, they are beginning to rebuild the tombs. Many generations are buried here. Some graves are several hundred years old. My family bought burial space before Liberation. My grandfather is buried here. This is my mother's grave; she died in 1984.

There was a period when dancing was not allowed, but now it has been revived again. People come to the graves twice a year. The other time is the first or second day of the 'Spring Festival' (Chinese New Year), but they don't fix the graves then, they just visit."

87

88. 供奉食物给祖先。
89. 清明节，一家人围着一座新坟跳舞。
88. Offering food to the ancestors
89. Dancing around a new family grave during the "Qing Ming Festival"

89

The Dongba Culture in Lijiang
丽江县的东巴文化

90. 丽江东巴文化博物馆东巴和学文（译音）。

和学文："我是在父亲的教导下成为一名东巴的。那时，我们家族里已经有五六代人都是东巴。我正式学习东巴知识是在 12 或 13 岁，但是在这之前，我早已看着父亲做东巴法事好多年了。我 18 岁时，如果有人请我，我已经能自己实践了。当我第一次出去做东巴法事时，我已能做仪式的一些部分，剩下的部分由父亲来做。

我们没有一种能取得东巴资格的考试，但是，有一个重要的法事，它由一个杰出的东巴来组织，有许多其他的东巴参加。在这个仪式中，决定一个人是否能成为未来的东巴，他必须有能力恰当地主持法事。这取决于看他能否完成他在这个仪式中必须完成的法事。我父亲做东巴已经 70 年了，他是个很好的东巴。正如所有的喇嘛都必须去拉萨学习一样，所有的东巴都必须去白地（今中甸县三坝乡白地村）学习，但实际上仅有极少数的人去过。我父亲就去过。

过去，最重要的仪式都与病痛和死亡有关。病的原因是由恶鬼引起的，有些法事是使病人摆脱恶鬼。我们认为有两种死亡：自然的和非自然的。东巴所扮演的角色，是上天堂路上的灵魂护卫者。非自然死亡是由事故、自杀或者凶杀引起的。有一种死亡也被认为是非自然的：如果亲属们、朋友们和邻居们在死者咽气前没有到场，或者，确信没有人死前举行过特定的仪式。在这种情况下，东巴举行仪式，使非自然死亡转变为自然死亡。

东巴们必须学习读和熟记许多仪式的经文，所有的经文都是纳西象形文字。现在，训练有素的东巴越来越少。有些自称东巴，但他们自知不是训练有素的东巴，因此不敢主持仪式。

在刚解放那个时期，我不得不放弃东巴这个职业，当时已不允许我们开展'迷信的习俗'活动。更糟的是在'文化大革命'时期，当时我被叫做'批判对象'。我经历了 30 个非常艰难的年头。之后，在 1981 年，东巴研究所成立后，我被邀请去那儿工作。我再三拒绝，我不想去。1990 年，我最终被说服了，到博物馆来工作。虽然有 40 年我不当东巴了，但东巴知识还留在了我的记忆里。

我有三个儿子和一个女儿，我是从泰安来的一个农民，我不想让任何一个儿子再做东巴，我害怕他们没有能力以此谋生。

90. Dongba He Xuewen, Lijiang Dongba Cultural Museum

He Xuewen:

"My father taught me to be a Dongba. By that time there had been five or six generations of Dongbas in our family. I began to study formally at the age of twelve or thirteen, but I had already been watching

90

my father for years. By the time I was eighteen, I could practice on my own, if someone asked me to. When I first started out, I would do a few parts of the ceremony; my father would do the rest.

There is no examination to qualify you as a Dongba, but there is an important ceremony, organized by a prominent Dongba and attended by many other Dongbas. Here, it is determined whether or not the prospective Dongba can properly carry out the ceremonies he must be able to perform. My father was a Dongba for 70 years, and a very fine one. Just as all Lamas must go to Lhasa to study, all Dongbas must go to Baidi, but very few of them actually go. My father is one who did.

In the past, the significant ceremonies were related to illness and death. Illness was thought to be caused by demons, and there were ceremonies to rid the sick person of demons. We considered that there were two kinds of death: natural and unnatural. The Dongba's role was to escort the spirit on the road to heaven. Unnatural deaths were those caused by accident, suicide or murder. A death was also considered to be unnatural if the right relatives, friends, and neighbours were not present or if certain ceremonies were not performed prior to death. In these cases, the Dongba could perform ceremonies to convert an unnatural death into a natural one.

Dongbas have to learn to read and memorize great numbers of ceremonial documents, all in Naxi pictographs. Now the number of trained Dongbas is fewer and fewer. Some people who call themselves Dongbas know they are not well enough trained, so they will not perform ceremonies.

 I had to give up being a Dongba at the time of Liberation, when we were no longer allowed to carry out "superstitious practices." It was even worse during the Cultural Revolution, when I was named a "struggle object." I was about 36 at that time. I was sent for "reform through labour" and had to do the worst work. I went through thirty very difficult years. Then, in 1981, when the Dongba Research Instiute was formed, I was invited to be a Dongba there. I refused. I didn't want to. In 1990, I was finally persuaded to work here at the museum. So for forty years I wasn't a Dongba, though it remained in my memory.

I have three sons and one daughter. I come from Taian and am a farmer. I didn't want any of my sons to be Dongbas. I was afraid they would never be able to make a living."

91

91. 东巴和学文（译音）在用一头黑猪做祭品来安抚恶鬼。
92. 东巴和学文（译音）指着表示四季的象形文字：冬天（雪）、春天（风）、夏天（雨）、秋天（花）。在每个符号下面，都有一个"3"，上面一个月亮；月亮在上面代表天。

　　黑板的右边是和志为，他在东巴研究所学习过，他每周两次教两个班，年龄在9—10岁孩子们学习纳西象形文字，在目前为止，在丽江学校教育系统里，这是惟一的一个班。

91. Dongba He Xuewen performing the sacrifice of a black pig to pacify demons
92. Dongba He Xuewen points at pictographs of the four seasons: Winter (snow), Spring (wind), Summer (rain), and Fall (flower). Below each symbol, a "3" and a moon; above, the pictograph for heaven. Standing to the right of the blackboard is He Zhiwei, who studied at the Dongba Research Institute. He teaches Naxi pictographs twice a week to two classes of nine and ten year olds. So far, this is the only such class in the Lijiang school system.

92

93. 简单的象形文字和译意。
94. 在丽江黑龙潭公园的一个宗教场所。
95. 在丽江东巴文化研究所,东巴何开祥(译音)和何积贵(译音)在研究纳西东巴手写稿。何开祥老人已经77岁,何积贵老人73岁,他们可能是惟一能完全看懂老的东巴经文的人了。第一批100卷被翻译成汉文的象形文字经典,最近已经出版,这是纳西人拯救这种神圣知识的举措。
96. 盲东巴和成德(译音),正在吹奏"葫芦笙",这件乐器是用葫芦制作的(丽江)。

和成德:"我3岁的时候就失明了,8岁开始学习东巴知识,现在56岁了,从没有结过婚。

有时我能从神灵那儿获得力量,虽然东巴们不是国王,但是东巴能解决人神和人鬼之间存在的问题。"

93. Sample pictographs with translations
94. A sacred site at the Black Dragon Pool Park
95. At the Dongba Culture Research Institute in Lijiang, two Dongbas, He Kaixiang and He Jigui, are studying a Naxi Dongba manuscript. Both men are 76 years old and most likely the last Dongbas able to fully understand the old scriptures. The first 50 volumes of translations of these pictograph writings have recently been published in an attempt to save this sacred knowledge. The next 50 volumes are expected to be published in the year 2001.
96. He Chengde, a blind Dongba, playing a 'Hulusheng', an instrument made of a gourd, Lijiang

He Chengde:

"I became blind when I was three years old and began to learn to be a Dongba, when I was eight. Now I am 56 and never married. Sometimes I can get the power from the gods. Dongbas are not kings, but Dongbas can manage the problem between the gods and mankind, between demons and mankind."

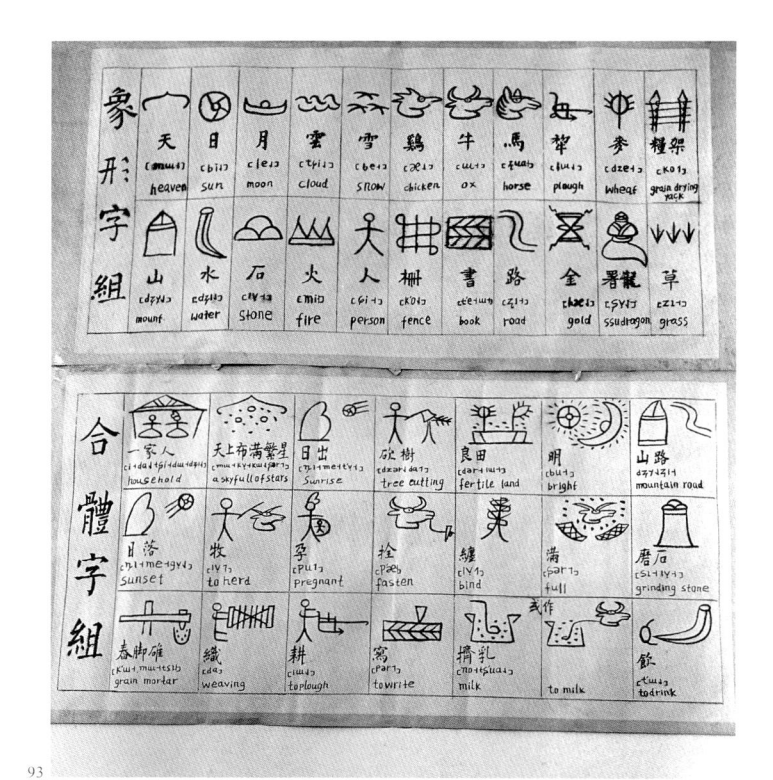

95

96

The Dongba Culture in Baidi,
Zhongdian County

中甸县白地的东文化

97. 纳西婚礼歌。
"明亮的星星闪耀在这吉祥的日子,
在'古仔'的家中,
父亲和儿子日夜忙碌。
远处是宽阔的草原,
田地耕种得很肥沃。
七百只白色的山羊绕着圈子转,
在这七百只羊中有一只很突出,
它有着可爱的斑点,
它象征着幸运吉祥。
由于命运福气,她被邀加入这个家庭。
父亲坐在左边,浑身充满着幸福,
母亲坐在右边,满脸洋溢着喜悦。
新娘新郎结合后九个儿子将出世,
他们的努力将创造出九块新的天。
新娘新郎结合后将生出七个女儿,
从她们这儿将开出七块丰收的地。
我们多么幸运!
神圣、富足、繁荣昌盛!"。
——(由老东巴苏银甲(译音)吟唱)

在白地附近的布弯村举办的和继全(译音)和赵秀云(译音)的婚礼上,一位80岁的老东巴苏银甲(译音)和另外几位村里的长者, 在新郎父母的家,为这对新人唱祝福歌。

97. Naxi wedding song
"The stars are well aligned on this auspicious day;
 In the Gu Zai family, father and son are busily working away.
On one side, wide grasslands over there,
On the other side, fields fertilized with care.
Seven hundred white goats are milling about,
But among the seven hundred, one stands out,
The one with the lovely beauty mark,
The one with the symbol of good luck,
Because of fate and felicity,
She's invited to join the family.
The father's side sit on the left,
happy through and through,
The mother's side sit on the right, and they are happy, too.
Nine sons will be born after bride and groom are mated,
And through their efforts,
nine new heavens will be created;
Seven daughters, too,
this marriage will yield,
And from them will come seven new crop fields.
How lucky are we!
Blessed and wealthy,
Thriving in prosperity!"
As chanted by Dongba Shu Yinjia and the elders

Naxi wedding song, The wedding day of He Jiquan and Zhao Xiuyun at Buovan village, near Baidi, Zhongdian county. Shu Yinjia, an 80 year-old Dongba, and other village elders chant blessings on the bride and groom in the family room of the groom's parents' house.

98. 和继全（译音）和赵秀云（译音）为参加婚礼的客人们敬酒。
99. 为了婚礼的盛宴，这家人杀了一头牛、一头猪和二十只鸡。大多数鸡都是村民们送来的礼物。村民们互相帮助是这里的传统。
100. 在一整天咏唱以后，东巴苏银甲（译音）为第二天在白水台献祭的仪式作准备，他正在木桩上写东巴象形文字。
101. 白水台位于白地村上面，是东巴文化和庆典的圣地。

98. He Jiquan and Zhao Xiuyun are toasting the wedding guests
99. For the wedding feast, the family killed one cow, one pig and twenty chickens. Most of the chickens were gifts. Village people support each other, that is the tradition.
100. After a long day of chanting, Dongba Shu Yinjia writes pictographs on wooden slats for next day's sacrificial ceremony at Bai Shui Tai (the White Water Mesa).
101. Bai Shui Tai above Baidi village is a shrine for Dongba culture and ceremonies.

100
101

102. 两位东巴正在咏诵祭天的象形文经书。
103. 东巴象形文字。
104. 一头大黑猪是作为去祭天的供品，猪头放在树下的石头平台上，与供奉的大米饼、酒、茶、面粉、谷物和酥油放在一起。
105. 猪肉切碎后分成相等的份数放在树叶上，分送给村民们。他们等着叫到自己的名字后去取肉。

102. Two Dongbas lead the chanting apropriate for the "Sacrifice to Heaven" ceremony from a pictographic manuscript.
103. Naxi pictographs
104. A large black pig was killed as a sacrifice to heaven, and its head placed on a stone platform under a tree, along with offerings of rice cakes, wine, tea, flour, grain and butter.
105. The pig's meat, cut up and placed in equal portions on a bed of leaves, is distributed to the villagers, who, plastic bags in hand, are waiting for their names to be called.

104

105

106. 阴历二月八日是祭奠"三多自然之神署"的日子。和学义（译音）带着两只鸡去白水台祭奠。

很久以前，三多自然之神与人类是兄弟。三多是哥哥，人类是弟弟。后来，他们分了家，90%的自然归三多，10%归人类。人们不能随便出外砍树、割草，否则三多便会用疾病来惩罚他们。人们没有办法，请丁巴什罗（东巴教的创始人）来解决问题。

丁巴什罗问三多的孩子们，"署"什么时候从水中出来（因为"署"住在水里）。他们说阴历每月的初一、十五"署"从水中出来。

丁巴什罗派大鹏神鸟"修曲"在阴历初一那天在东边等着"署"，当"署"浮出水面，他看到了（大鹏神鸟"修曲"）立即钻进了水里。在阴历十五那天，"修曲"神鸟坐在西边。"署"从水中出来，没有看到大鹏神"修曲"，便开始洗头。突然大鹏"修曲"猛扑过去抓住了"署"，并说要杀了他。"署"说："如果你杀了我，这儿就没有水和草原了。"大鹏"修曲"说："我不在乎，我不喝水也不吃草，只需要肉和血。"

这时，丁巴什罗来到这儿。他假装不知道他们打架的事，他问："这儿发生了什么事情？""修曲"告诉他说，90%的自然属于"署"，只有10%归人类。丁巴什罗劝说"署"，把90%的自然给人类，留下10%归自己。"署"也把他的黑玉给了丁巴什罗；这就是为什么黑玉属于人类的原因。

尽管自然神"署"只拥有10%的自然，但这10%非常重要，它就是水和自然。

——以上的故事由盲东巴和承德（译音）讲述。（丽江）

107. 东巴苏银甲（译音）供奉一只装饰过的公鸡给神。仪式过后，公鸡将被放生。

106. February 8th of the Lunar calender is the day of "Sacrifice to Ssu, the God of Nature". He Xueyi is taking two hens to the celebration at Bai Shui Tai.

Long, long ago, Ssu, the God of Nature, and mankind were brothers. Ssu was the older brother and mankind the younger. Later they divided their household: 90 percent of nature belonged to Ssu and ten percent to mankind. People could not go out to cut trees or grass, or Ssu would punish them and put illness on them. People had no way out, so they invited Dongbashiluo (the founder of Dongba religion) to manage the problem.

Dongbashiluo asked the children of Ssu at what time Ssu would come out of the water (because Ssu lives in the water). They told him that Ssu comes out of the water every first and fifteenth day of the lunar month.

Dongbashiluo sent Xiuqu (Sacred Rock) on the first day of the lunar month to wait for Ssu on the East side, When Ssu came out of the water, he saw Xiuqu and went back into the water. On the fifteenth day of the lunar month Xiuqu was sitting on the West side. Ssu came out of the water and did not see Xiuqu. He began to wash his hair. Suddenly Xiuqu flew over and caught Ssu and told him he would kill him. Ssu said: "If you kill me, there will be no water and no grass." Xiuqu said: "It doesn't matter, I don't drink water and I don't eat grass, I only need meat and blood."

Then there came Dongbashiluo. He pretended that he knew nothing about the fight and asked them: "What happened?" Xiuqu told Dongbashiluo that ninety percent of nature belongs to Ssu and only ten percent to mankind. Then Dongbashiluo persuaded Ssu to give ninety percent of nature to mankind and keep only ten percent for himself. Ssu also gave his black jade to Dongbahsiluo; this is why black jade belongs to mankind.

Though Ssu now only owns ten percent of nature, those ten percent are very important, because it is the water, it is the nature.

As told by He Chengde, a blind Dongba, Lijiang

107. Dongba Shu Yinjia offers a decorated rooster to the god to ride on. After the ceremony, the rooster will be let loose.

107

108. 年轻的小伙子们正带着供奉的木牌和鲜花，走在白地白水台的泉华台地上。
109. 年轻的姑娘们也走向祭坛。
110. 手拿着刀的村民们把鸡血奉献给"署"神。
111. 这个小池塘是"署"神的家，人们向"署"神供奉新的木牌，饵块、钱和粮食。

108. Young men are walking up the wet, white mesa with offerings of wooden slats and flowers.
109. Young women, too, make their way up to the shrine.
110. Knife in hand, villagers offer the blood of their chickens to Ssu.
111. The well and small pond, the home of Ssu, has been given new wooden slats and offerings of rice cakes, money and grain.

110

111

112. 10个东巴来到这儿，表达他们对自然之神"署"的敬重。
113. 在白水台的泉华台地上，许多家庭安营扎寨，享受野炊的快乐。
112. Ten Dongbas have come to pay their respect to Ssu, the God of Nature.
113. Everywhere on the mesa, families have settled down to cook and to enjoy the day.

113

The Naxi and Mosuo people
of Yongning, Ninglang County
宁蒗县永宁的纳西人和摩梭人

114

114. 神圣的格姆山（宁蒗）。

　　达巴阿翁托丁（译音）："格姆（译音）是一位非常美丽的摩梭女子，能织奇妙的麻布。她爱上了丽江的玉龙雪山。丽江的大山也常常来看她，他们有一种走婚的关系。

　　同时，另一个叫布纳（译音）的男人也爱上了格姆，他用一根绳子拴住了她。格姆伤心地哭了……
　　她的眼泪变成了泸沽湖。"

114. The holy Genmu mountain

　　Ddaba Aweng Tuoding:

　　"Genmu was a very pretty Mosuo woman who could weave wonderful hemp cloth. She fell in love with the Jade Dragon Snow Mountain in Lijiang. The mountain in Lijiang often came to see her; they had a walking-marriage relationship. At the same time, another man named Buna, also fell in love with Genmu, and he used a rope to tie her up. Genmu was sad and crying. Her tears became the Lugu Lake."

115. 泸沽湖。
116. 贾阿丁曾（译音）和他的儿子、在拉罗畹村附近。

贾阿丁曾："我和一位摩梭女人有过走婚关系，我有个儿子在温泉附近的村子里。因为家里需要个女人，我请求她的家里人允许她到我们村里来和我一起生活，但是她的家人不同意，所以我放弃了，并找到了另一个普米女人，和她结了婚。这是我们的儿子，我认为一个人年轻的时候，走婚还可以，但是人渐渐地老了，最好还是住在一起。"

115. Lugu Lake
116. Jiaadingzeng with his son, near Laluowan Village
Jiaadingzeng:

"I had a walking-marriage with a Mosuo woman in a village near the Hot Springs and I have a son there. Because my family needs a woman, I asked her family to allow her to come to my village and live with me, but her family did not agree, so I gave up and found another woman, a Pumi woman, and married her. This is our son. I think that when a person is young, it is alright to have a walking-marriage, but when a person gets older, it is better to live together."

116

117. 阿米宾玛·次尔拉措（译音），家庭的女家长（巴奇村）。

118. 阿妮普提（译音）和阿妮大都（译音，永宁）。
阿妮大都："我有6个孩子。一个在昆明工作，一个准备做喇嘛在西藏学习，一个女儿嫁给了纳西人，一个在丽江工作，还有一个儿子、一个女儿和我生活在一起。他们都还小，还没有情人。等我有了孙子，这个院子会更热闹一些。我妹妹有一个情人，可几年前他去世了。

我和丈夫生活在一起。我们是走婚关系，但在文化大革命期间政府说：'一夫一妻制'。所以他来到我家和我一起生活，我兄弟也去了情人家和她住在一起。我兄弟已经死了。

在摩梭地区走婚是人们正常的风俗。有的人一生只有一个情人，有的人常常换情人。如果他们彼此不再相爱，分手时也不会感到不高兴，如果只是有一方变了心，另一方会感到非常伤心。

我年轻的时候，很多年轻的小伙子爱我，但我都不愿意。惟独有一个小伙子请人上门来和我妈谈，我妈认为这个家伙不错，我决定与他建立爱情关系，他就成了我孩子们的父亲。一个走婚的男人，没有必要每天去那个女人家。如果在母亲家里有事做，他就和家人在一起；如果女方的家里很忙，他也能来帮助他们。

如果我看到孩子们常常换情人，我会劝说他们静下来，选择一个长期的情人，但最终这种事还是由他们自己决定。我不在乎结婚还是走婚，只要他们幸福就可以。"

117. Amibinmo Cierlacu, the matriarch of her family, Baqicun Village

118. Ani Puti and Ani Dadu, Yongning Ani Dadu:

"I have six children. One works in Kunming, one is learning to be a Lama in Tibet, one daughter married a Naxi, one works in Lijiang, and one son and one daughter live with me. They are still young, so they have no lovers. The courtyard will be more lively when I have grandchildren. My sister had a lover, but he died quite a few years ago.

My husband lives with me. We had a walking-marriage, but during the Cultural Revolution the Government said: 'One wife and one husband,' so he came to live with me in my family, and my brother went to live in his lover's house. But my brother died.

In the Mosuo area people normally have the custom of the walking-marriage. Some people have a lover for their whole life; some people change their lovers very often. If they no longer love each other, they will not feel unhappy separating, but if only one of them has a change of heart, the other will feel really sad.

When I was young, a lot of young men wanted me, but I refused. Only when a man sent a person to my house to talk to my mother, and my mother thought this man was a good guy, did I decide to have a love relationship with him. He became my children's father. When a man has a walking-marriage, it is not necessary for him to come to the woman's house every day. If he has work to do at his mother's house, he stays with his family, and if the women's family is really busy, he can come to help them, too.

If I find my children changing lovers very often, I will persuade them to calm down and choose a long-term lover. But in the end it has to be their own decision. I don't care whether they will marry or have a walking-marriage, as long as they are happy."

117

118

119

119. 阿米宾玛（译音）家的全家福：次尔拉措和她的兄弟，喇嘛；两个儿子和一个女儿，一个孙女和三个重孙。

120. 杨学侯（译音）和他妻子木国蓉（译音，永宁下开基村）。

木国荣（译音）："我的老家是丽江的七河村，丈夫的老家是丽江的束河村，我们俩都是在永宁出生和长大的。我父亲和祖父是皮匠，祖父是从军队里逃到永宁的。

过去我们住在永宁的皮匠村，但是1956年，我们和其它10家人搬到了这个地区，剩下的人重建了房子，我有许多亲戚住在这儿。

村里不是所有的人都是从军队里逃出来的，有的是来做生意留下的。皮革生产很受当地人的欢迎，甚至有一些藏民从四川木里来买皮革。

我们夫妻俩是裁缝，主要做摩梭服装，一般是丈夫裁剪我缝制。过去我们有一个商店，但是现在人渐渐老了，身体也不太好，我们仍然在家做一些服装。"

119. Portrait of the Amibinmo family: Cierlacu with her brother, a lama; two sons and one daughter, one granddaughter, and three great-grandchildren.

120. Yang Xuehou and his wife, Mu Guorong, Xiakaiji Village

Mu Guorong:

"My hometown is Qihe Village of Lijiang, my husband's hometown is Shuhe village of Lijiang. Both of us were born in Yongning and we grew up here. My husband's father and grandfather were leather craftsmen; the grandfather came to Yongning to escape the military.

In the past we lived in Leather-Craftsmen village. But in 1956 the headman of Yongning, who at that time was Vice-County-Governor of Ninglang (put into this position by the Communist party but not in support of it), organized some Mosuo and Yi people to burn down the Leather Craftsmen village. That is when we, and ten other families, moved to this area. The remaining people rebuilt their houses. I have many relatives who live there.

Not all the people in that village came to escape the military; some came only for business. The leather products were welcomed by the local people and even some Tibetans from Muli in Sichuan would come to buy.

My husband and I both are tailors. We mainly make Mosuo clothing. Usually my husband cuts, and I sew. We had a shop before, but we are getting old and our health is not so good. We still make some clothes at home."

121. 杨文贵（译音，永宁）。

杨文贵："我是纳西人，是丽江县石鼓镇人。我在永宁中学当了30年的教师。现在退休了。

有许多纳西人住在永宁，大多数都住在皮匠村。他们的上一辈是1920年从军队里逃出来的，都是从事皮革生产的，但是现在再也没有人做这个工作了。他们中有的人和摩梭人结了婚。"

122. 阿坝旦诗玛（译音，大普窝村）。

阿坝旦诗玛："纳西和摩梭语非常相似，只有极少数的纳西语我们不懂。有句老话说：'摩梭、纳西、藏人死后骨灰将会在一起'。"

123. 和自才（译音，永宁皮匠村）。

和自才："我父亲是丽江大研镇的头人，纳西人。我1948年出生，在我两三岁时父亲就死了。我记不得他长得什么样子，对他也没有特别的感觉。我母亲是摩梭人，他是父亲家的佣人，后来我出生了。父亲死后她找了一个摩梭男人生了我妹妹。他是我的邻居。

因为我是地主的儿子，不能参军，过去也找不到工作，所以我是个农民。但是做农民挺好，我的仓库里有很多粮食，楼梯上挂了很多火腿。有些城里人看不起我们，但他们不可能像我们这样，拿得出那么多火腿来。"

124. 和自才家客厅的装饰。

和自才："在墙上挂毛主席的像很时髦。如果我们不在这儿挂他的画像，还能挂什么呢？"

121. Yang Wengui, Yongning

Yang Wengui:

"I am a Naxi, I come from Shigu town of Lijiang County. For thirty years I have been a teacher at the Yongning Middle School. Now I am retired. There are a lot of Naxi people living in Yongning. Most of them live in the Leather-Craftsmen Village. Their ancestors came in the 1920s to escape the military. They were all engaged in leather production, but at present nobody there works with leather any more. Some of them got married to

Mosuo women."

122. Aba Dangshima, Dapuo Village

Aba Dangshima:

"The Naxi and Mosuo languages are quite similar; only a few words of the Naxi language we cannot understand. There is an old saying:'Mosuo, Naxi and Tibetan's bone ashes will come together after they die, but not with the Yi people.'"

123. He Zicai, in Leather-Craftsmen Village,

Yongning

He Zicai:

"My father was the Headman of Dayan town of Lijiang, a Naxi. He worked for Jhiang Kai-shek. In 1951 or '52 he was killed by the Communist Party. I was born in 1948, so I was two or three years old when my father was killed. I cannot remember what he looked like and I have no special feelings for him. Maybe he really was a bad man. My mother is a Mosuo, she was a servant at my father's house, and later I was born. After my father died she found a Mosuo man and my sister was born. They are my neighbours.

Because I am the son of a landlord, I could not join the army, I could not find a job in the past. So I am still a farmer. But being a farmer is good. I have all kinds of grain in my storage room and many hams hanging upstairs. Some city people look down on us but it is impossible for them to take out a lot of hams, like we do."

124. He Zicai's living-room decoration

He Zicai:

"It's just a fashion to have Chairman Mao's picture on the wall. If we didn't put his picture there, what else could we put up?"

125. 孩子们在忠实完小（靠近永宁的一所小学）。
126. 索纳米阿妈（译音）有几个孙子在家里吃饭（永宁）。
125. Children at the Zongshi Wanxiao, one of the primary schools near Yongning
126. Suonami Ama, feeding some of her grandchildren in the family room, Yongning.

125

126

127.

127. 在索纳米（译音）家"老房子"的午餐时间。1987年索纳米家分家了，因为35个人同住在一个家里人太多了。

　　就这样，有"老家"，过了街是"新家"。年龄小的孩子们现在在两个家来回走，家里和田间的工作也由两家共同分担。

128. 索纳米·纳宗（译音）大妈是"新家"的女家长，正在捆稻草做草垫子（永宁）。

127. Lunch time at the "old home" of the Suonami family The Suonami family divided in 1987 because there were 32 members, too many people for one household. Thus, there is the "old home," and a "newhome" across the sreet. The small children now go back and forth between the old peopleof both households. Work is also shared between the two households.

128. Suonami Nazongduma, matriarch of the "new home," bundling the straw for making a mat, Yongning

128

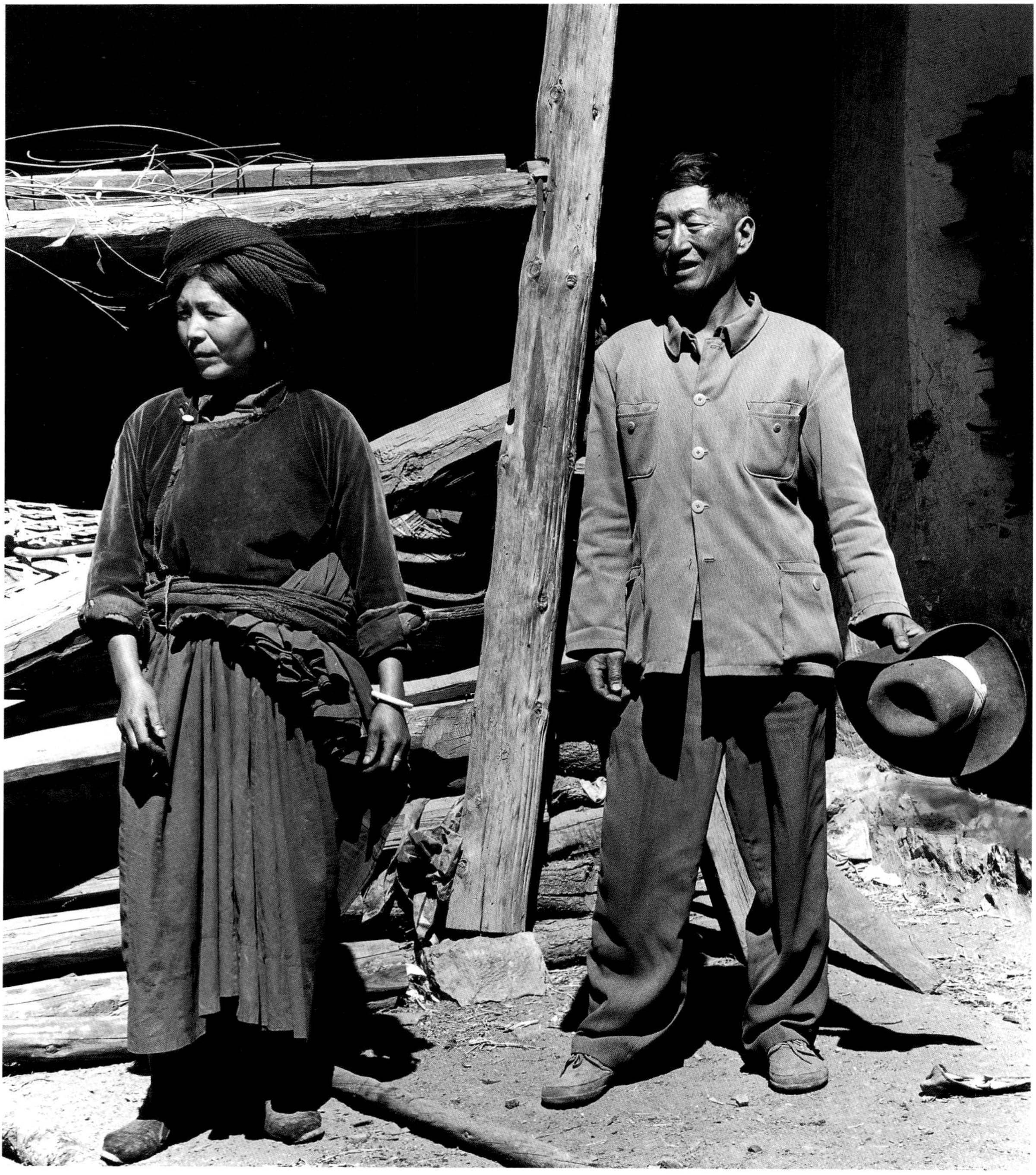

129

129. 索纳米·拉措（译音）和茹萨次尔（译音）。

索纳米·拉措："自'文化大革命'以后，茹萨次尔和我生活在一起，他两年前死了。我喜欢走婚制，因为，所有出生于同一个家庭的人都住在一起，都来自母亲的家庭。当一个家庭成员做了错事，我可以立即直言不讳地指出来。如果是媳妇，她来自另一个家庭，用同样的方式和她交谈就不容易了。

我母亲现在84岁了，掌管一个家庭对她来说太老了。现在我决定一切，但如果我做错了什么事，家庭成员可以指出来并且告诉我怎么改正。我母亲也会纠正我。

我自己选择孩子们的父亲。在摩梭社会一个男人找情人我们叫做'米实（译音）'，女人找情人我们叫做'盼金若实（译音）'。情人们相互称呼他们自己的名字。现在，政府有一条规定：女人必须在20岁，男人在24岁才允许找情人生娃娃。但是有些年轻人十七八岁就有情人了。政府说如果他们在20—24岁前怀孕，就罚款。但到目前为止，没有一个人被罚款。

做一个家庭的母亲是非常累的事，但是所有家里最艰苦的工作都是为了孩子们，所以没有什么问题。"

130. 索纳米纳宗独玛（译音），抱着她的重孙。

索纳米达娃："如果你想了解摩梭人，我认为你最好先了解摩梭妇女、母亲、老人。老人们和孩子们从她们的家庭里得到许多的爱。当奶奶给孩子喂奶——当然她没有奶水，但是这表示她把最强烈的爱给孩子们。我的奶奶就是这样照顾我们的。

129. Suonami Lacuo and Rusa Cier

Suonami Lacuo:

"Rusa Cier lived with me since the Cultural Revolution, but he died two years ago. I like walking-marriage, because all the people living in the household come from the same family, from the mother's family. When a family member does something wrong, I can speak out immediately. If there is a daughter-in-law, she is from a different family and it is not easy to talk to her in the same way.

My mother is 84 years old now, too old to manage things in my family. Now I make all the decisions, but if I did something wrong, a family member will point it out and tell me how to do it right. My mother also will correct me.

I chose my children's father by myself. In Mosuo society we call a woman looking for a lover 'Panjinruoshi,' and a man looking for a lover, we call 'Chumishi.' The lovers call each other by their own names. At present, the government has a regulation whereby a woman has to be twenty and the man 24 to be allowed to find lovers and give birth. But some young people begin to find a lover when they are seventeen or eighteen years old. The government says that if they are pregnant before they are 20 and 24 years old, they will be fined. But so far, no fines at all.

To be the mother of a family is very hard work. But all the hard work is for my own children, so it is no problem."

130. Suonami Nazongduma, holding a great-grandchild.

Suonami Dawa :

"If you want to understand Mosuo people, I think you'd better understand the women, the mother, the old people. The old people and the children get much love from the family. When the grandmother takes care of her grandchildren, she gives her breast to the children, though she has no milk. But it shows a strong love for the children. My grandmother took care of us this way."

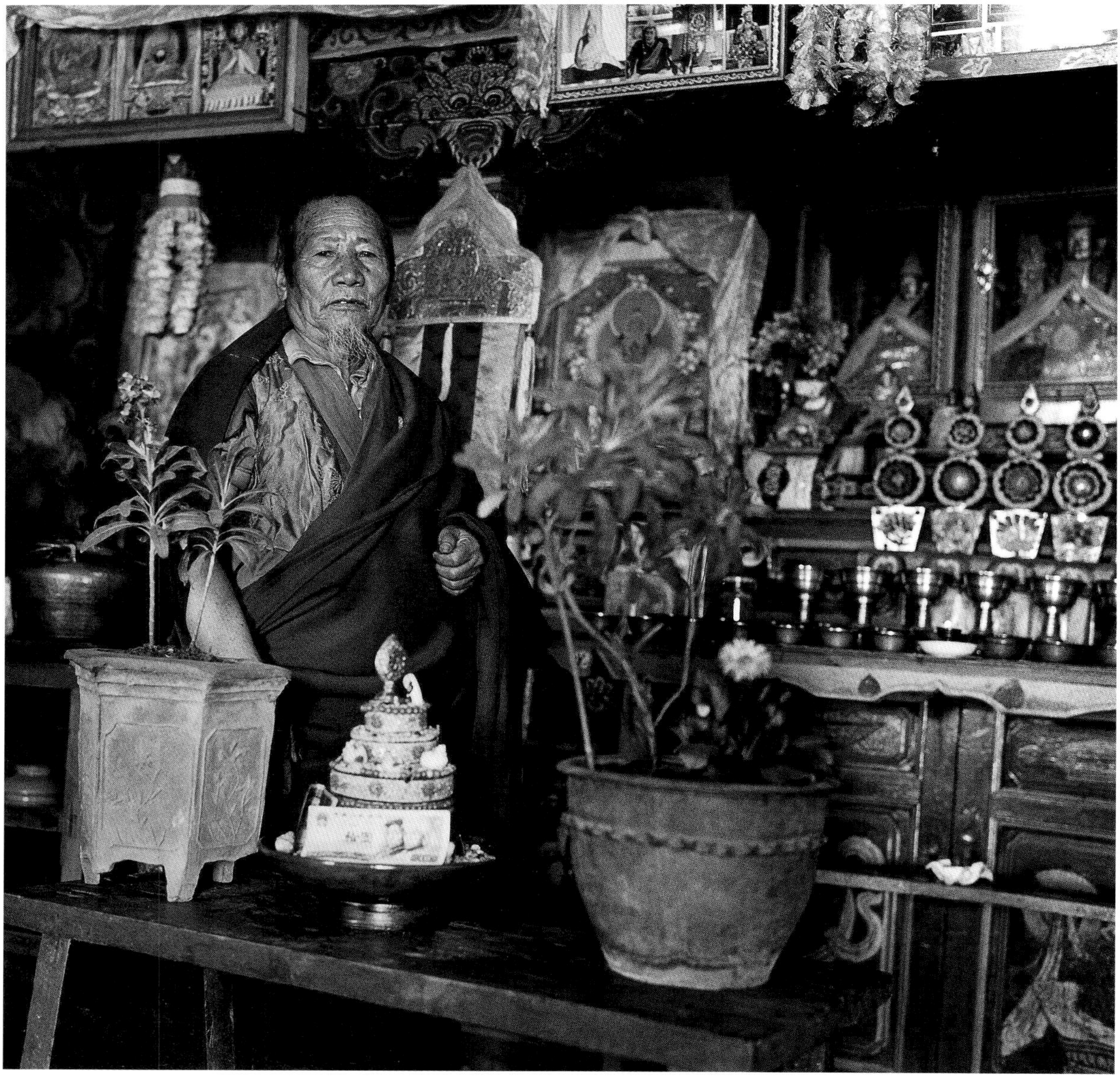

131

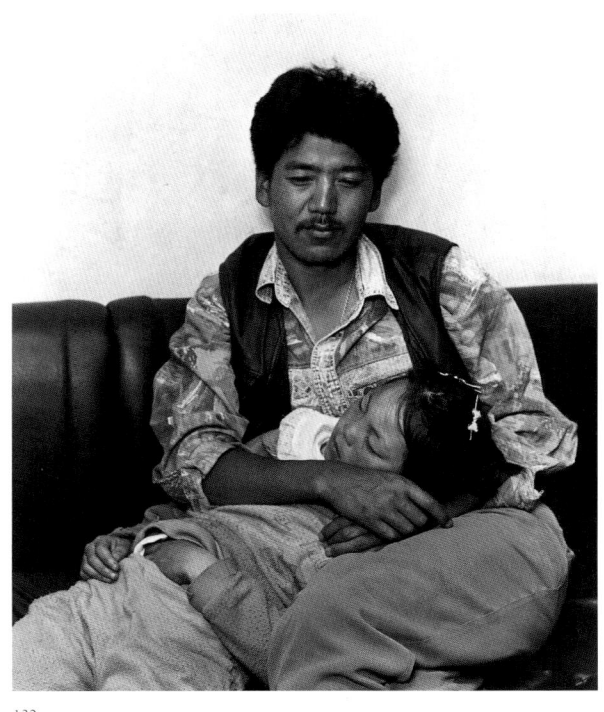

132

131. 喇嘛哈尔巴（译音）在索纳米"老家"的祭坛。

喇嘛哈尔巴："我18岁时去了拉萨，在那儿住了10年。我是走着去的，走了4个月。所有的喇嘛都必须去西藏。如果你不去，你永远是个'小喇嘛'，你必须在拉萨通过考试。一旦通过了第一次考试，你就像一只羽毛丰满的小鸟一样可以自己飞了。我自从28岁离开拉萨后再没有回去过。我住在这儿，我的工作不需要我到别处去。我们常常被请到很远的地方去做法事。"

索纳米达娃（译音，喇嘛的侄子）："他每年的收入比我高。喇嘛们得到很多捐款。但在内心里他只是一个佛教徒。如果你问他要一分钱做别的事，都会遭到拒绝。他也有很多的花销：佛经非常贵，并且有许多册；点灯的酥油30元一斤；他还要捐赠钱给寺院，为塑大佛付钱。他也花钱去拉萨。这房间的一部分也花了不少钱，他用了50年时间才装饰成这么高的水平。"

132. 索纳米达娃（译音）和他的侄女小花花。

索纳米达娃："对我来说最幸福的时刻是，我收工回到家，我的小侄女给我端来热茶和热水洗脚。"

索纳米拉措，他的母亲："我们摩梭人不像汉人叫'爸爸'这个特别的词，我们叫爸爸和舅舅用同一个词'阿乌'"。

131. Lama Haerba in his sanctuary at the "old home" of the Suonami family

Lama Haerba:

"I went to Lhasa at the age of eighteen and stayed there for ten years. I walked. It took me four months. All lamas have to go to Tibet. If you don't go, you remain a 'xiao lama'. You have to pass examinations in Lhasa. Once you have passed the first examination, you are a fully fledged lama. I have not gone back since I left at 28. When my services are not reqired elsewhere, I live here. We are often asked to perform ceremonies far away."

Suonami Dawa, the lama's nephew:

"His yearly income is much higher than mine. Lamas are given many donations. But in his heart is only Buddhism. If you ask him for a penny for anything else, he will refuse. Also, he has many expenses. Scriptures are expensive, and there are many volumes. Yak butter for the lamps costs 30 RMB per jin (a pound). He donates money to the temple, he paid for one of the big statues. He also sends money to Lhasa. This is the part of the house on which most money has been spent. It has taken fifty years to reach the present level of decoration."

132. Suonami Dawa with his niece Xiao Hua Hua

Suonami Dawa:

"The happiest time for me is when I come home from a day of work and my little niece offers me some hot tea and brings me hot water to wash my feet."

Suonami Lacuo, his mother:

"We Mosuo people have no special name for 'father' like Han Chinese do, we call father and uncle with the same word, 'Avou'."

133.

133. 喇嘛崔推塔奇（译音，永宁）。

喇嘛崔推塔奇："我是从嘎拉村来的，是普米族。我们村一半普米一半摩梭。我18岁做了喇嘛，22岁去西藏。我在那儿呆了38年，38年间我只回来过两次。

两年前，我在永宁街上开了这间小藏医诊所。这个地区大多数人还很穷，西药太贵，藏药也很贵，当有人来请我治病时，如果他们没钱，我会免费给他们药。当然，有时候碰到有钱的人，他们会多付一点儿钱。我相信佛教和藏药关系很密切，为了永宁人民我会把它们结合起来。

许多人患有一种心脏病，是想得太多而得的病。首先，你应该吃药；第二，吃些好东西；第三，有些好朋友，他们会给你带来幸福。"

134. 阿巴旦诗玛（译音）和她的女儿阿巴金若拉姆（译音）在她们的院子里（大坡村）。

阿巴金若拉姆："我兄弟昨天去情人家了，今天没回来，因为他的情人家有很多农活，所以他留下来帮忙。他有两个孩子，都与母亲生活在一起。"

阿巴旦史独芝（译音，阿巴旦诗玛的兄弟）："解放前，我们没有稻田，永宁的头人不允许我们种稻子。他担心如果外面的人知道我们这儿能种稻子，他的土地会被人夺走。他非常有钱，是靠剥夺老百姓的财富发家的。"

阿巴旦诗玛（译音）："是的，这个头人很坏。他很注重自己的穿着，穿得很好。他不允许普通老百姓穿好的。普通老百姓经过他的门前，必须脱掉鞋子或者摘掉头上的装饰，要不然他就打他们。"

阿巴金若拉姆（译音）："我听外婆和母亲讲，大坡村的头人有两个妻子，一个是丽江人，另一个是本地的，她们经常为金、银或其它的财宝而打架。丽江那个比较漂亮，生了个女儿。但是本地的那个没有孩子，老百姓说，是因为她对人太残酷。"

133. Lama Cuituitaqi, Yongning

Lama Cuituitaqi:

"I come from Gala village. I am Pumi. My village is half Pumi and half Mosuo. I have been a lama since I was eighteen years old and went to Tibet when I was 22. I stayed there for 38 years. During those long 38 years I came back only twice.

Two years ago I opened this small Tibetan medicine clinic here, on Yongning Street. Most people in this area are still very poor and western medicine is very expensive; so is some Tibetan medicine, but when people ask me to cure their disease and they have no money, I will give them medicine free of charge. Of course sometimes rich people will give me much more. I believe that Buddhism and Tibetan medicine are closely related, and I want to bring them together for the people of Yongning.

Many people have a kind of heart disease which comes from thinking too much. You first take the medicine; second, eat good food; and third, have good friends who will bring happiness to you."

134. Aba Dangshima with her daughter Aba Jinruolamu in their courtyard, Dapuo Village

Aba Jinruolamu:

"My brother went to his lover's home yesterday and won't come home today because his lover's family is busy with their farming, so he stays there to help them. He has two children; they live with their mother."

Aba Dangshiduzhi (Dangshima's brother):

"Before Liberation we had no rice fields. The headman of Yongning did not allow people to grow it. He worried about people from outside taking his land away if they knew we could grow rice here. He was very rich. He became rich by taking away common people's wealth."

Aba Dangshima:

"Yes, the headman was very bad. All he cared about was having good clothes. Common people were not allowed to dress well. When common people passed his gate, they had to take off their shoes or their headdress, or else he would beat them."

Aba Jinruolamu:

"I heard from my grandmother and my mother that the headman of Dapuo village had two wives: One was from Lijiang, and the other was local. They often faught with each other for gold, silver, or other treasures. The one from Lijiang was quite pretty. Later she had a daughter, but the local one had no children. Common people said the reason was that she was too cruel to the people."

134

135

136

137

135. 大坡村的房子。
136. 大坡村的稻田。
137. 犁地准备种包谷（大坡村）。
135. Houses at Dapuo Village
136. A rice field at Dapuo Village
137. Preparing the field to plant corn, Dapuo Village

138. 阿巴旦诗玛（译音，大坡村）。

阿巴旦诗玛："过去，我家所有的布都是我织的。那时候，衬衫、裙子、裤子、任何东西都是用大麻织的。他们也用不同的纤维织厚的毯子、毡子。

我织腰带，它也能作绑脚用。我也织装谷子的口袋和其它的东西。过去我把所有的时间用来织布，现在我们有许多另外的事情要做，所以，我为我家的喇嘛们织一些东西。无论如何，每个月我都去永宁的喇嘛庙两次。"

139. 独玛（译音，76岁，拉志村），和她的朋友们到永宁的扎美喇嘛寺。

独玛："我每个月来这儿3次，带些食物给喇嘛们，并且烧香、点灯。从我的住处到这儿要走2个小时。"

138. Aba Dangshima, Dapuo Village

Aba Dangshima:

"In the past I was weaving all the clothing for my family. In those days, shirts, skirts, trousers, everything was made of hemp. They also wove with different fibers to make rugs and blankets. I am making a belt. It can also be used as wrapping for the legs. I also make bags for grain and other things. I used to weave all the time. Now we have too many other things to do, so the few things I weave are for the lamas and for my family. I go to the lama temple in Yongning at least twice a month."

139. Duma, aged 76, of Lazhi Village, with her friends at the Zha Mei Lamasery in Yongning

Duma:

"We come here three times a month. We come to bring some food for the lamas and to burn incense and light lamps. It is about a two-hour walk from where we live."

138

139

140

140. 永宁扎美寺的节日。
　　喇嘛："这个寺庙有很长的历史，在"文化革命"期间它被毁了。只有一座建筑留存下来，是藏医院的一个药品仓库。新的寺庙是10年前重建的。
　　今天是阴历9月20日，是佛教的节日。我们不知道汉语和摩梭语怎么说。每天我们都到这儿来，一直到25日为止。老百姓们也要来这儿做祷告，他们将带些小礼物来，比如大米、红糖、茶等。"
141. 瓦拉别村的夜晚。

140. A festival at the Zha Mei Temple
　　Lama:
　　"This temple has a long history, but it was destroyed during the Cultural Revolution. Only one building survived, it was the medicine storage room of the hospital at that time. The new temple was rebuilt about ten years ago.
　　This is September 20th according to the lunar calendar, the festival of Buddhism. We don't know how to say it in Chinese or Mosuo lauguage. We will come here every day until September 25th. The common people will also come here to pray. They will bring some small presents such as rice, brown sugar, tea, etc."

141. Evening at Walapian Village

142. 达巴阿翁拖丁(译音,瓦拉别村)用他的项链在一个小法事里,帮助一位妇女生孩子。

达巴:"我7岁时从爷爷那儿学做达巴,他是我妈妈的叔叔,我是家里的第四代达巴。我现在28岁,是永宁地区惟一的达巴。

平常我就在家里帮助家里干活,但是如果人们需要我,我就会帮他们主持法事。人们请我为他们修房子、盖新房、主持葬礼、为孩子们取名、杀猪或者结婚做法事。

摩梭人很少结婚,但是如果一户人家只有一个男人,家里需要个女人,女人应该在男人家安家。当我被请到一户人家给孩子取名时,我会考虑孩子母亲的出生日期和出生的方位。丧葬时,人们将请达巴去主持葬礼,同时也请喇嘛。在达巴和喇嘛之间没有竞争,我们各自吟诵自己的经文,不同的是语言,喇嘛颂经用藏语,普通的老百姓听不懂,他们懂达巴颂经,因为用的是摩梭语。

摩梭人信奉佛教,同时也信奉达巴教,过去在这个地区有很多达巴,达巴教很有权威,后来佛教变得更有权力。我们也有一个房间有佛教的供桌(祭坛)。我母亲在阴历的初一、十五都去永宁的喇嘛庙。有时我也去那儿点一个灯,但是我不参加喇嘛的活动,他们颂经用藏语,我听不懂。

达巴相信祖宗,相信山神、水神、火神等。摩梭人进食时,不管吃的是什么,首先,我们要向祖宗和火神祭献食物,放一些食物在供桌上或者一块特殊的石头前面,如果供桌上的食物太多,我们就把它给猪吃。

我们相信所有的树木和野生动物都属于山神,因此,当摩梭人盖房子需要砍树时,首先必须祷告和祭祀山神。如果是打猎,我们要祭祀山神,然后,我们就能够带走所需要的一些东西。但是,如今的年轻人不太在乎这些习俗了。这不好,山神将惩罚我们,人们将遭受灾害的惩罚。"

143. 达巴阿翁拖丁(译音)的书。

阿翁拖丁:"达巴没有经文,传说很久以前一个达巴去很远的地方学习经文。他把所学到的东西都写在了牛皮上,当达巴走回家的时候,他的肚子饿极了,找不到任何可以吃的食物,他便把牛皮煮了,并且全部都吃了。所以,所有的经文都在达巴的肚子里。

我有一本书叫做'格利木',是摩梭语的,它记录了一年的12个月。28个字母都是摩梭语,他们反复地用它。我爷爷教我怎么使用这本书,它是用来占卜那些特殊日子的。"

142. Ddaba Aweng Touding, Walapian village, using his necklace in a small ritual, helping a woman whose child is sick.

Ddaba:

"I learned to be a Ddaba when I was seven years old from my grandfather, who was my mother's uncle.

I am the fourth generation of Ddabas in my family. I am 28 years old now and am the only Ddaba in the Yongning area.

Normally, I stay at home to help my family doing labour work, but when the people need me, I will go to help them to hold ceremonies. People invite me to hold ceremonies for repairing their house, building a new house, holding a funeral, children's name-giving, killing pigs or marriage.

Not many Mosuo people marry, but when a household has only men, and the family needs a woman, the woman might settle down at the man's house. When I am invited to a family to give a name to a child, I take the mother's birthdate and the direction of birth into consideration.

When there is a funeral, people will invite the Ddaba to hold the funeral, at the same time lamas are also invited. There is no competition between the Ddaba and the lamas, we each do our own chanting. The difference is in the language. Lamas chant in the Tibetan language, which common people do not understand, while they understand most of the Ddaba's chanting. We chant in the Mosuo language.

Mosuo people believe in Buddhism, while also believing in the Ddaba religion. In the past there were many Ddabas in this area, and the Ddaba religion was really powerful. Later Buddhism became more powerful. My family also has a room with a Buddhist altar, and my mother goes to the lama temple in Yongning on the first or fifteenth day of the lunar month. Sometimes I go there to light a candle, too. But I don't take part in the lama's activities; they chant in the Tibetan language, and I don't understand.

Ddabas believe in ancestors, in the Mountain God, the Water God, the Fire God, etc. When Mosuo people eat food, no matter what it is, we first sacrifice to the family's ancestors and the Fire God. We put some food on the upper part of the tripod or on a special stone in front of it. If there is too much food on the tripod, we give it to the pig.

We believe that all the trees and wild animals belong to the Mountain God. Therefore, when Mosuo people want to build a house and need to cut some trees, we first must pray and sacrifice to the Mountain God. Or if we hunt, we sacrifice to the Mountain God. Then we can take some of the things we need. But nowadays, some of the young people don't care. It's not good. The Mountain God will punish us and inflict disaster on the people."

143. Ddaba Aweng Tuoding's book

Aweng Tuoding:

"Ddabas have no scriptures. It is said that a long time ago a Ddaba went to learn the scriptures at a place far away. All the characters were written on cowskins. When the Ddaba walked home, he felt very hungry but could not find any food. He cooked the cowskins and ate them all. So now the scriptures are in the Ddaba's belly.

But I have a book which is called 'Gelimu' in the Mosuo language. It records the twelve months of the year. The characters are Mosuo characters, 28 of them, and they are repeatedly used. My grandfather taught me how to use this book; it is for divining special days."

143

144

144. 达巴的母亲和侄女。

达巴："我们相信有来生。如果一个人做了许多好事他的来生一定还是一个人；如果他做坏事，他将变为一头牛或一个别的动物。他也可能最后变成人，但是需要很长的时间。

当我祖父快死的时候，我们预测过未来，得到了一个结果，说有个女孩将要来到我们家。真的，两年以后，我妹妹生了个女孩，我们相信这是祖父的灵魂转世，我们悉心地照顾她，就像祖父过去照顾我们一样。"

145. 达巴的一个友邻以及他的孙子（瓦拉别村）。

144. The Ddaba's mother and niece

The Ddaba continues:

"We believe in reincarnation. If a person did a lot of good things while he was alive, he will be reincarnated as a person again; but if he was not good, he will come back as a cow. It is also possible that the animal turns into a person, but it will take a long time.

When my grandfather was dying, we did future counting and we got a result saying that a girl will come to my family. Really, two years later, my younger sister gave birth to a girl. We all believe her to be the reincarnation of my grandfather and we take good care of her, as he used to take good care of us."

145. A friend and neighbour of the Ddaba with his grandchild, Walapian Village

146. 在嘎拉村的一个房间，一口棺材被陈列在家里显著的位置。

索纳米达娃："摩梭人认为死亡比出生重要得多。当一个人死了，她或他将被用白色的麻布包裹起来，呈胎儿的状态，并且按照她或他再生的方向葬在家里。喇嘛将被请去主持并且选测一个吉日火化。只有在火化的两天前，才将死人移进棺材里去。

这个女人76岁，她20天前死的。只要酥油灯还在燃烧，她的灵魂还在，明天是她的葬礼。"

147. 火炮枪连响三声和随之而起的鞭炮声宣告近亲的到来。走在前面的男人是死者的大儿子。

148. 他们请了18个喇嘛在屋子里颂经。

149. 大多数喇嘛在里面颂经，另外的在外面装饰酥油花。

146. At a house in Gala Village, a coffin is prominently displayed in the family room
Suonami Dawa:

"Mosuo people think that death is much more important than birth. When a person dies, she or he will be wrapped with white hemp into the fetal position and buried in the family's house according to the direction of her or his birth. A lama will be invited to chant and to calculate which will be the perfect day for the cremation. Only two days before the cremation will the dead person be moved into the coffin. This woman is 76 years old. She died twenty days ago. As long as the candles are burning, her life is not completed. Tomorrow will be her funeral."

147. Three gunshots and the sound of firecrackers announce the arrival of close relatives. The man in front, the oldest son of the deceased, will be in charge of the funeral.

148. Fifteen lamas have been invited to chant at the house.

149. While most of the lamas are chanting inside, others are preparing a decorated pastry outside.

148

149

150. 在嘎拉村附近的小山上，4个年轻的喇嘛正在准备火葬的场地，以便"向神祇祈求为死者买块地"。
151. 喇嘛们在准备葬礼的现场，亲属们为火化死者而堆了个柴堆。
152. 喇嘛们站在旁边，死者的大儿子察看场地。
153. 柴堆已经堆到了蔓荼罗的顶上。用于火葬死者，柴堆用的柴必须是单数。

150. Up on a hill, near Gala Village, four young lamas prepare the ground for the cremation: "To buy a place from the gods for a new house."
151. While the lamas are preparing the funeral site, relatives build a pyre for the coffin.
152. The lamas stand by as the oldest son takes over.
153. The pyre has been moved on top of the Mandala. For the cremation of a woman, it has to have an uneven number of logs.

152

153

154

154. 第二天清晨,三声枪响召唤大家帮助抬棺木到葬礼地点,随后将棺木放到火葬的柴堆里。人们对着棺木鞠躬、磕头,再对着喇嘛们磕头,然后离去。
155. 只留下几个家庭成员待到火化结束,火化后的死者将葬在这座大山里。
154. Early the next morning, three gunshots summon the men to carry the coffin to the funeral site and place it in the pyre. They bow to the coffin, bow to the chanting lamas, and leave.
155. Only a few family members remain, watching over the cremation. The bones of the woman will be buried in the mountains.

155

责任编辑：徐　芸　彭　晓
装帧设计：徐　芸
设计助理：向云波
翻　　译：菱　蔓　安　利

Duty Editor: Xuyun　Pengxiao
Layout　Designer: Xuyun
Asistant Designer: Xiang　yunbo
　Translator: lingman

我眼中和心中的形象
——生活在丽江、白地、永宁的人们
Sight and lnsight
—— Life in Lijiang, Baidi, and　Yongning
Ulli Steltzer

乌利·斯特尔兹 著　　菱　蔓　安　利译
出版发行：云南美术出版社
　　　　　（昆明市环城西路609号）
印刷：深圳雅昌彩色印刷制作有限公司
版次：2001年12月第1版
印次：2002年2月第1次印刷
开本：787×1092　1/16
印张：9
印数：1-3000
ISBN7-80586-848-4/G·122
定价：86.00元